CONTENTS

PASSING ON
THE MOVE OF GOD
TO THE NEXT
GENERATION

BERT M. FARIAS

PART II: PREACH THE WORD

PART III: PROJECT STEPHEN: A PORTRAIT OF A LAST DAYS PREACHER

THE LORD'S ENDORSEMENT

When my wife Carolyn and I prayed and laid hands on the manuscript of the book you now hold, she saw a blank page for the Foreword. We were about to submit it to a prominent minister to see if they would endorse the book, but the Lord arrested us. We were also thinking of multiple friends who could write short endorsements called "blurbs," but then, as we were praying and committing this literary work to the Lord, the vision and the following Spirit-inspired prayer utterance flowed through Carolyn's vessel.

"A Foreword from God is the highest endorsement, for He is the Most High. His words and what He wants to say about this book is the highest endorsement one could receive.

"For I see the image of a pastor passing on the baton of prayer to intercessors and pray-ers, so they could understand the move of God that first comes in prayer."

My comments:

In Jesus' earthly ministry and in the garden in His most trying hour, was not this life and anointing of prayer the most critical element the Master and Suffering Servant wanted to pass on to His disciples, too (Mt. 26:36-46)? Without this element of the spirit of prayer being passed on to those we teach and disciple, there will not be a strong foundation in them. If it's not in you, it won't be in them, because you cannot give what you don't have.

And at the Mount of Transfiguration, was it not the experience of being in the glory that He also desired to pass on to His inner circle of disciples (Mt. 17:1-9)? Without experiencing the glory of God's presence, what will the next generation have?

And in Jairus' house, was it not again in the mind of Christ to impart the miracle-working spirit to His closest disciples (Mk. 5:21-23; 35-43)? What is Christianity without miracles?

The next generation must experience all of these things, not in theory but in reality. The baton of the move of God in prayer, power, and the glory and anointing of the Holy Spirit must be passed on.

Carolyn continues:

"I also see Elijah and Elisha and the passing on of a double portion of the anointing from the elder to the younger according to the plan and purpose of God (2 Kings 2:8-15).

And I see Joshua standing at the tabernacle (Ex. 33:11) waiting for the impartations of the move of God.

It's a move! It's a move! The move of God is the fruit of the words of this book.

I see altars filled with people waiting…and waiting…and lingering in the presence and move of God.

Is this not a book about Your wisdom? Is this not a book about following You? Then who shall we listen to but You and Your words?

Talk about an endorsement! Who else would you want to endorse your book?

And so I feel so strongly (tongues) about the Scripture for this book: "For that which is born of God overcomes the world, even our faith" (1 Jn. 5:4).

For this book was born of God, so carry it now, Father; carry it all the way through to the birthing — through the doors, through the utterances, and through the moves of God that I now see.

Let it be placed in the hands of those who are Yours — men and women of the Spirit.

And so now we place it in Your hands, Father, to carry it through for what is ahead.

So let it give birth to that which is of the Spirit and born of God.

Let it give birth to those who are spiritual and those who are godly, and those who are walking with You to pass on — to pass on the Spirit and the Word. Let there be an understanding and a doing of it for a reproduction and a multiplication through them."

SCRIPTURES

"Oh God, You have taught me from my youth; and to this day I declare Your wondrous works. Now also when I am old and gray-headed, oh God, do not forsake me until I declare Your strength to this generation, Your power to everyone who is to come" (Ps. 71:17-18).

"And the things that you have heard from me among many witnesses, commit these to faithful men who will be able to teach others also" (2 Tim. 2:2).

PREFACE

Now, well into the 21st century, we have reached a crisis in the Pentecostal/Charismatic movement. Although there have been many good ministries birthed in the last few decades, with them also have come a deluge of unsound beliefs, erroneous practices, and extreme and excessive teachings, along with a glaring absence of the moving of the Holy Spirit and a diminishing of the real power and presence of God.

From a defective and cross-less gospel, to a dumbing down and a cheap imitation of the ministry and work of the Holy Spirit, to the gross overemphasis on personal prophecy and prophetic ministry, to New Age gobbledygook and psychic themes, to a hollow "apostolic" movement, we have witnessed an entire spectrum of unfruitful cycles of spiritual junk.

When the Holy Spirit, through the apostle Paul, foretold of the departure from *"the faith"* (1 Tim. 4:1), and in a similar admonition wrote through Jude to *"contend earnestly for the faith"* (Jude 3), He was not referring to saving faith but to the entire corpus of New Testament Christianity, which entails doctrine, experience, belief, and practice. In other words, when the Holy Spirit speaks of *"the faith,"* He is referring to the entire package of Christianity.

Too many of us have lacked the wisdom, neglected the light, and failed to pick up what our godly forefathers and spiritual giants passed on to us and instead have built weak "spiritual" sandcastles that will not pass the test of time and whose quicksand will suck down its victims.

Many of us have been unskillful at taking the old and blending it into the new. We have neglected the ever-increasing light of the revelation of the Word and the genuine flow and true manifestations of the Holy Spirit from the past and failed to bring them into the new. Some have stayed in the candlelight of the truths of centuries past. Others have moved on from the candlelight age to the lantern of a brighter glow of Spirit and truth. But the wise householder has combined the foundation of the progressive light of the Word of God from days of old and the pure, strong move of the Holy Spirit to bask now in the light of God's greater glory (Mt. 13:52).

A Facebook friend of mine wrote me the following concerning the Word and the Spirit that men of old carried:

"The men and women of old knew nothing of the extensiveness of error in the cotton-candy gospel of today. They nipped it in the bud. They stated without apology that without holiness we won't see the Lord. They knew Scripture far better than today's Bible professors. Sister Pauline Parham, the daughter-in-law of Charles Parham, told me in Dallas in the early 1980s that the old preachers knew the Word far better than the new generation, and powerful moves of the Spirit not seen today were common." (Charles Parham [1883-1929] was the first preacher to articulate Pentecostalism's distinctive doctrine of evidential tongues and to expand the movement.)

Like the days of old when the new temple was being built in the time of Haggai, while the young men were rejoicing in what they thought was a great glory, the old men wept because it did not compare with the former glory they knew.

"But many of the priests and Levites and heads of the father's houses, old men who had seen the first temple, wept with a loud voice when the foundation of this temple was laid before their eyes. Yet many shouted for joy..." (Ezra 3:12).

The weeping of the old men was probably a result of the disappointment over the temple's lack of splendor compared to that of Solomon's temple.

Is this attitude not being repeated today when the younger who were not a part of the great past moves of God boast of the glory of the Lord that is incomparable to what the older have witnessed? In fact, to those who've experienced the former, the "new" or the latter, is as nothing in their eyes.

"Who is left among you who saw this temple in its former glory? And how do you see it now? In comparison with it, is this not in your eyes as nothing?" (Hag. 2:3)

All hope, however, is not lost, for the promise of the Lord, indeed, is that the glory of the latter house will be greater than the former.

The following prophecy, given to F.F. Bosworth's (1877-1958) granddaughter concerning the ministry of her grandfather's day, gives us hope for the greater glory to be restored to the Church[1] once more.

"The ministers of your grandfather's day lit a Pentecostal fire that swept the world in their generation, but that fire has now died down to where only ashes and embers are left. But I am going to use your grandfather's recordings to breathe on these embers with the wind of My Spirit, and that fire will rekindle and sweep the world again in a new Pentecostal revival."

It is my earnest prayer that, from the pages of this book shall emerge a pattern and a blueprint of the Spirit's cry for a glorious Church and for a generation of ministers and saints who will possess a balance of His Word and His Spirit in power and demonstration. In the final section of the book, you will be presented with a portrait of a new breed of a last-days preacher.

My hope is that the publishing of this work will effect a rekindling of holy zeal for authentic revival and reformation in our day.

May the baton of the glory of the move of God be passed on to ensuing generations.

---

1   The word 'Church' is capitalized throughout the book to denote the Universal Church, otherwise it is left lower case to refer to the local church.

PART I

THE DEMONSTRATION OF THE SPIRIT AND POWER OF GOD

CHAPTER 1

THE WISDOM OF MEN *VS.* THE WISDOM OF GOD

In the 1980s and into the '90s, there was a great wave of a move of God's Spirit that was rising and gaining momentum in the American Church, but somehow it was miscarried and never reached its full potential. The reason for this was a gradual and subtle attachment to man's wisdom that crept in. Preeminence was placed on outward appearance, and the goal for so many pastors and churches became numerical growth and money — attendance, giving, and protecting their own projects.

I was blessed to have been a part of the end of the Charismatic movement and, later, a great outpouring of the Holy Spirit known as the Brownsville revival. In the latter, I witnessed how the reputation of man eventually became more important than the glory of God, resulting in the full effects of that outpouring and its lasting long-term fruit being aborted.

I also witnessed the ugliness of religious politics and the precedence it gained over the bond of love under which the leaders of that revival had previously labored — thus, the reason for the subsequent diminishing of the Spirit of God in that great revival. This seems to be the pattern of revivals throughout history. When men stop following after love and start politicking and being more concerned about denominational distinctions and man's agenda than they are about the purposes of God, the flow and power of the Spirit is also cut short.

Today, as more and more of our Spirit generals and pioneers are departing to their eternal reward, I see a greater dependence being placed on the wisdom of men. If men are unwilling to pay the price to wait on the Lord for His plan and His higher wisdom that would produce the wine of the Spirit, then they will naturally lean to man's wisdom and the wine of the flesh.

I've seen the effects of so many churches over the years that are using man's methods to market their programs and projects, maintain and increase their membership, and keep "business" open. I have concern for conferences that train pastors and leaders to run their churches like CEOs run their businesses and companies. I see an attachment to pretty things, and messages for the sweet tooth that take the offense away from the gospel. What kind of example are we setting for the next generation?

"For who shall bring the presence of God but those who understand the Spirit of God? And herein is a part of the equipping of the body — to understand this (spiritual) place. For there is such an effort and assault against who we are in Christ and what He paid for. And that is why there are people so disturbed by what is going on with "making things easy" for people to come into our churches. It goes against the very core of what Jesus died and paid for. So many, like sheep, are just following the latest fads/trends because they have the outward form of godliness but deny the power. How can men see the wisdom of God unless they be in the Spirit?" (Holy Spirit-inspired utterance)

Spiritual leaders must bring understanding to these things so that revelation will come to many hearts and God's people will begin to press into a greater place in the Spirit instead of consulting their souls. The Spirit of the Lord has borne witness of this problem in that many of His leaders and people consult their souls far too much, thus limiting their access into seeing the manifold wisdom of God, which is first spiritually discerned (1 Cor. 2).

There is an evil spirit working to diminish and take away the manifold wisdom of God from the Church (Eph. 3:10), and we must contend for the victory in this matter. The victory and glory of God, and the heavenly places where we are seated is enough for the Church to stand in this hour and to bring this wisdom forth.

"However, we speak wisdom among those who are mature, yet not the wisdom of this age, nor of the rulers of this age, who are coming to

nothing. But we speak the wisdom of God in a mystery, the hidden wisdom which God ordained before the ages for our glory, which none of the rulers of this age knew; for had they known, they would not have crucified the Lord of glory" (1 Cor. 2:6-8).

The rulers of this age (Satan and his cohorts) were completely confounded by the wisdom of the cross. It was an upside-down plan. The quality of this wisdom is foolishness to the natural man. For example, those ministers who are walking closely with the Lord in this hour are doing the opposite of what man's wisdom would tell them to do to grow a church or a ministry. The early Church grew numerically through the wisdom and power of God, not through fads and trends and the methods of men. God uses the foolish things to confound the wise.

The blood of Jesus is over those saints in this spiritual place who seek to understand His plan for this hour. Deception shall not win.

We will stand and fight in the name of Jesus for that place in the Spirit so that His body will understand and His manifold wisdom can be displayed before the principalities and powers of this world.

"This should be the vision and commission of every minister — to go to that place of prayer so that provision can be made of the wisdom of God for the body of Christ. Spiritual men understand this, and they seek it. This is why wise men seek those who pray and have a place with Me — because they know that the wisdom of God is the highest standard." (Holy Spirit-inspired utterance)

THE POWERS OF THE AGE TO COME: A HOLY SPIRIT-INSPIRED UTTERANCE

"So many of My people follow the wisdom of men in a man, a personality, who do not move in the Spirit and the powers of the age to come because there are few who minister in this, My standard. And so the absence of ministers of the true Spirit has created a void for My people to follow ministers of the flesh, who move only in the wisdom of men.

But how will they follow My wisdom and power in a man, and how

19

will they follow the powers of the age to come unless they sniff the scent of it, and taste the edibleness of it, and see it, and bear witness to it? For it is not just in a healing or a prophecy that My Spirit manifests Himself; for is it not written of My Son that His works were so many that volumes of books could not contain them? And have you not heard of your fathers and generals I gave you, and of the wonder and diversity of My works and My powers that were witnessed in days of old and generations gone by?

But how will My people begin to desire these powers and believe Me for these powers except they be manifest? For it is when these powers are on display and they are manifest that then those who taste them and bear witness of them will begin to desire for more, pray for more, and believe for more. And there will be a great stirring of hunger, desire, and of faith and expectation from which I will respond.

But who will pave the way except those who've heard of these things, and who know these things, and who've been trained in a measure in these areas? And how will these powers of the age to come be brought forth except through prayer that gives birth to these things? And how will My ministers step out in these things unless they move out in faith? For even as you've heard of My servant who started that school and who taught you (speaking of the late Kenneth E. Hagin), was it not to separate the flesh churches from the Spirit churches? Was not My established purpose to divide and distinguish ministers of My power and of My Spirit from those of the flesh, and to impart the knowledge and the understanding, the faith, and the boldness to step out and step forth into these things?

But there must first come a moving into prayer. There must first come a high esteem for that holy place of communion with Me. Into that room and closet must you first enter, and then there will be a moving up into that realm where I am and where you see and know. It is then that these things shall be birthed. The many distractions must be put aside, just as those who've followed ministers of the flesh, as they witness the real, will cast aside earthly wisdom and go after Me and the ministry of the Spirit.

To know that the powers of the age to come and My greater glory not yet witnessed by this generation can come forth in greater manifestation only through prayer is to esteem that place above all others. To those who do, I will show Myself strong, and their labor of prayer and their delight in My communion will surely bring forth their heart's desire for the powers of the age to come and for My glory to be in greater display and manifestation.

So there has to be a moving into and then a moving up so that there can be a moving on. For little progress has been made in the realm of the Spirit where the wisdom of men has ruled and prevailed. But now it is high time for those who've been taught and trained and moved in some of these things to move into a greater fullness, for the hour is late and the need so great."

CHAPTER 2

FLESH CHURCHES *VS.* SPIRIT CHURCHES

As guardians of local churches, shepherds have been entrusted with such a great responsibility. They can be either a lock or a key to opening the door to the move of the Spirit of God in their midst. The Word of God is our foundation, but the Holy Spirit supplies the life. The more we follow the leading of the Spirit, the greater will be the life flow in our meetings and times of assembling, and, of course, in our personal lives as well.

The only way to see a turnaround in many local churches today is to focus first on personal and leadership renewal and then on congregational renewal. Let everything else be subservient to that order, including our mission and structure. What happens, though, is that we usually work this in reverse. We establish our mission and structure and then attempt to breathe life into it, instead of following the life and direction of the Spirit of God and then facilitating that life with the necessary structure. There is a world of difference between these two approaches. Unless renewal happens first, all else is in vain.

These two approaches are like the difference between a powerboat and a sailboat philosophy. A powerboat runs on the human fuel of education, leadership books, programs, going to seminars and conferences, and fine-tuning systems of the church, but a sailboat is dead in the water if the wind doesn't blow. Being a sailboat is difficult for the program-oriented, "bigger is better" American-culture activist, but it is the only way to glory.

The Church of the Lord Jesus Christ is a Church of holiness, love, and power. It is the workings of the Holy Spirit in the lives of His ministers and saints that makes it that way.

There are basically two types of churches today: Flesh churches and Spirit churches. A flesh church reaps death and corruption, but a Spirit church reaps life and peace (Rom. 8:6). Churches that revolve around the wisdom of men, social activities, entertainment, and carnal fellowship are flesh churches. They have the glitter, but it's not gold. They have fake glory and smoke, but there's no real fire. They may look good outwardly, but there's no internal depth and substance. Churches that are birthed and built through Holy Ghost prayer and the wisdom of God are Spirit churches.

Holy Ghost praying is the doorway to the supernatural. A few years ago, an interesting survey was taken to determine how often Spirit-baptized Pentecostal/Charismatics utilized their prayer language and spoke in tongues. Results showed that only 15% used their prayer language daily and only another 7% weekly. Nearly 50% never use it.

No wonder we have so many flesh churches.

Why do I mean by Holy Ghost prayer? Praying with your own understanding is mental praying, which is limited to the realm of your own mind and reasoning. Praying in tongues is praying with God's understanding, which is unlimited and often comes with interpretation and revelation (1 Cor. 14:14-15).

Another survey was taken among 50 Spirit-baptized Pentecostal/Charismatic ministers. Only 10% of them prayed at least 15 minutes a day in the Holy Ghost. No wonder so many are being diverted by the wisdom of men. No wonder there's so much showboating and fleshly preaching among ministers. Eloquent speech and persuasive words of man's wisdom have trumped the demonstration of the Spirit and power of God.

There is an entire breed of churches that are ignorant of how the Holy Ghost works and moves. Many teachers are teaching the way of the flesh instead of the way of the Spirit.

There simply will not be much profit without Holy Ghost praying. Who would've believed that one prayer group of 120 people in an upper room could've changed the world? God's plan for revival has not changed. The pattern was set long ago. God changes the world through abiding, persistent, and consistent Holy Ghost praying.

"The earnest (heartfelt, continued) prayer of a righteous man makes tremendous power available [dynamic in its working]" (Jam. 5:16b – Amp.).

I heard someone say one time, "The acid test of New Testament revival is the Church. And the acid test of the Church is prayer." The quickest way to kill churches is to let up on Holy Ghost praying or remove it altogether.

To say it another way, the spirit of prayer is the spirit of revival. The revival spirit leaves churches when Holy Ghost prayer meetings diminish or shut down. Revival returns when Holy Ghost praying returns. There is no other way. Prayer begets revival, and revival begets more prayer. Let us not complicate the message of revival. It starts and is maintained with Holy Ghost prayer, of which the larger part is praying in tongues often with interpretation, and with intercessions, groanings, and travail.

Satan has weakened and decimated churches through weakening the prayer life of Christians in their homes and in their churches. Many churches still don't have prayer meetings, and of those who do, they are the weakest and least attended of all meetings. There is little to no Holy Ghost praying that goes on. And of those who do have prayer, much of the praying is mental praying and not spiritual praying.

Once a Christian or a church lives in abiding Holy Ghost prayer, then it must obey the great commission and be about the Father's business of advancing the kingdom of God. Preach the gospel. Sow the seeds of the Word of God. Reach out to your community. Sow the testimony of Jesus Christ. Heal the sick, and cast out devils as Jesus commanded (Mk. 16).

This is the standard and pattern of revival for every church. This is revival made plain and simple. This is what every church and

Christian must be doing until Jesus comes.

Many churches are losing Pentecost as the early Church knew it and the Holy Ghost designed it. We are living in a day when man's reputation has become more important than God's glory. Social status, education, and the wisdom of men are more highly esteemed than the wisdom of God and the power of God.

When I asked an 85-year-old Pentecostal minister the reason for a lack of power in the Western Church today, he pointed to education as the biggest reason, citing Europe and America as the two greatest examples. This is where the wisdom of man has its roots. Unsanctified intellect has robbed the Church of spiritual life and power.

One foreign minister offered a very telling response after he had visited some of the largest churches in America and was asked what impressed him the most: "How much she has been able to accomplish without God." We have conceded to natural means found in the wisdom of man to advance the cause of Christ.

Pentecostals and Charismatics need to return to their Holy Ghost-and-fire roots. And all mainline denominational and evangelical churches need to go to their upper room and receive their baptism of power with the evidence of speaking in other tongues. Without tongues, you can never engage in real spiritual praying. That is how the move of God will grow.

CHAPTER 3

THE REAL CURE FOR SOCIETY'S ILLS:
MORE SPIRIT-AND-FIRE CHURCHES

One day Satan asked himself a question:

"How can I destroy America? No army can defeat them. Their economy is foolproof. They're geographically isolated and cannot be invaded. I know what I'll do. I'll get them through their children. I'll erase the commandments, the godly traditions, the family, morality, ethics, truth, and decency."

We are seeing this today in increasing proportions.

Then, while pondering on this evil, hellish strategy, Satan says:

"If I can get the Holy Spirit out of the Church, I can really take over."

And so there you have it — a spiritual laboratory analysis of what is presently happening in America. I wonder which evil strategy is the worst. Are you more concerned about what is happening in the nation or in the Church?

My concern is not as much for the nation, or the government, or the evils that have befallen our society because I understand that an evil, decadent society is never a match for the glorious, Spirit-filled Church.

Jesus walks among the lampstands (churches — Rev. 2 and 3). His concern is for the state of His Church. Although God is concerned about governments and His Word exhorts us to pray for all those in authority, for kings, presidents, governors, and such (1 Tim 2:1-2), there is hardly a mention found in the New Testament of the evils prevalent in a nation, a society, or the government. No word from the New Testament writers on Nero, Herod, or any ruling Caesar. No complaints about wicked governments, criticisms about wicked kings, how evil society was, or the state of failing economies. No attention was given to any of these issues. The Church and the spiritual health and welfare of the saints have always been the issue. Jesus wants His lampstands to burn bright.

As long as we are in this world, there will always be sin and evil. Nations, societies, and governments are made up largely of unregenerate sinners. Sinners are dead in their trespasses and sins. They are possessed by a sinful nature that makes them slaves to sin. Until they come to Christ and are born again, they are powerless to overcome the ravages of sin.

A strong spiritual Church burning brightly in the midst of a decadent society is our only hope. The true Church is the voice and moral conscience of a nation, and a restrainer of sin and evil.

The mind of the Spirit that the early apostles possessed was for the Church to be salt and light in society and to impact it through its character, power, and authority. A Church full of the Holy Spirit and reflecting the glory of God will affect any society. But to actually change society, you must change the hearts of the individuals within it.

The power and testimony of a transformed life and a heart on fire speak louder than any old tradition, new program, perfected logic, polished sermon, or eloquent speech. Give the local church a few burning testimonies of changed lives, and it can start to impact a city.

"Come see a man who told me all things that I ever did" (John 4:29).

Where is the power of the Spirit-inspired testimony in the Pentecostal/Charismatic and evangelical churches? It is only the effectual working of God's power in a human heart that will allow a man to go outside of himself and share the gospel boldly and testify of Jesus. *"In order to stop me, you've got to kill me,"* is the battle cry of the radically transformed man.

"For we cannot but speak the things which we have seen and heard"

(Acts 4:20).

When the saints of God are spiritually healthy and vibrant, it brings light into the local church and city. So precious are those who are on fire for Jesus, especially in times of gross darkness and moral decline as we are in now. Heaven takes note of them, and they shall shine as the stars forever.

"Those who are wise shall shine like the brightness of the firmament, and those who turn many to righteousness like the stars forever and ever" (Dan. 12:3).

In a time of spiritual declension in Great Britain in the 1800s, Catherine Booth, wife of Salvation Army founder William Booth, went about the churches *"looking for burning words."* She recognized that doctrine alone is not enough. Logical-sounding phrases and great swelling words are not enough. Oratorical skills are not enough. We must have the Word on fire and the power and move of the Holy Spirit.

Many churches need to get out of the twilight zone of cessation theology and postmodernism, and learn what it means to be filled with the mighty Holy Spirit and press on into all the fullness of God (Eph. 3:19).

While there are pockets of revival throughout certain parts of the nation, there has also been a disturbing trend in many Pentecostal and Charismatic churches of a lack of emphasis on the work, power, and fullness of the Holy Spirit. Listen to the words of the late John G. Lake, that great apostle to South Africa:

"I believe that the first essential in a real Holy Ghost church and a real Holy Ghost work is to begin to surround the baptism of the Holy Ghost with the reverence due an experience so sacred and so terribly costly."

The gospels and the book of Acts portray the original blueprint for the operation of the real Church. She was born in Spirit and fire (Acts 2:1-4) and can thrive only in the same. Yes, thrive even in the midst of a morally declining and grossly dark, decadent society.

Imagine if all Pentecostal/Charismatic churches caught fire. Imagine if all evangelical churches did, too. The impact on our nation would be unprecedented.

More of the workings and fullness of the Spirit is what we need — and fire, fire, fire on the churches of Jesus Christ!!!

CHAPTER 4

ABANDONING THE MACHINERY OF MINISTRY

The assembling of the Church should be a place where people seek God in faith, prayer, and expectation. There ought to be an awe and a reverence of coming together corporately into God's presence. The Scripture tells us that even sinners should be convicted by the presence of God in our midst.

"But if all prophesy, and an unbeliever or an uninformed person comes in, he is convinced by all, he is convicted by all. And thus the secrets of his heart are revealed; and so, falling down on his face, he will worship God and report that God is truly among you" (1 Cor. 14:24-25).

The apostle Paul lays out instructions for maximizing the power and presence of God in our gatherings. If things are arranged according to the Spirit's order and plan, He will be present and manifest, and people will be drawn to Jesus. Conversely, nowadays, church leaders study demographics and people's preferences in order to make the assembling of the church more appealing to them.

When we try to make church appealing and pleasing to man, it actually detracts from the presence of God and His plan and purpose. Conversely, when we organize our church agenda and gatherings toward pleasing God and according to the order of the Spirit, it is then that men will be drawn to Jesus.

Here is a simple equation for this:

Please God = Draw people

Please people = Detract from God

Building the church to cater to people's preferences does not draw the presence of God. God knows what people need far more than we do. Following His plan and purpose is what manifests His presence and power. The greatest meetings are those where we follow the leading and direction of the Spirit of God.

Years ago, there was a far-greater emphasis on making the church assembly appealing to God. There was a greater reverence for God and a caution not to grieve the Holy Spirit or quench what He wanted to do and how He wanted to move.

Today it appears we are so busy curtailing the church experience to accommodate what we feel people want or what we think they will respond to. So much care and thought go into not offending the people, but so little consideration goes into not offending God.

We tone down the Scriptures on sin and God's demands for true discipleship.

We arrange the music around what makes people feel good and happy, loved and accepted.

We program our services so as to not go past a certain time.

The standard that determined early Church policy was pretty clear.

"If anyone speaks, let him speak as the oracles of God. If anyone ministers, let him do it as with the ability which God supplies, that in all things God may be glorified through Jesus Christ, to whom belong the glory and the dominion forever and ever. Amen" (1 Pet. 4:11).

We do demographic studies and research people's preferences to make people feel comfortable and loved in church, cause them to return, and to know we are relevant. But God's wisdom is much higher and so much more effective.

What if God doesn't want them to feel comfortable? What if feeling comfortable is the root of their problems? Perhaps if people were allowed to feel uncomfortable, they would seek God for His comfort.

Instead of trying to show them that we care, what if knowing God cares is the only thing that can change them and set them free?

And shouldn't they return to church because they've had an encounter with God? And is relevance really that important when sin and spiritual blindness are the sinner's main problem?

The more we try to build God's house with our own efforts and in our own wisdom, the more we will labor in vain because we will attract people only to us and our programs. But if we let the Holy Spirit build the house, He will actually attract people to Jesus.

This recent Facebook post from a pastor friend says it all:

"There must be an abandoning by our preachers and churches from what someone called the 'machinery of ministry.' The status-quo, hold-down-the-fort type of thinking is killing the Church. We are sorely in need of a return to a supernatural Church comprised of spiritual initiatives and radical faith. We need to slay this manmade ministry that has been born out of cultural and social compromise.

"I believe we are headed for a time of 'pastoral clarity,' in which leaders are going to experience epiphanies of just who they are and who they are not. Pastors will quit trying to be all things to all people and instead will embrace being that 'one' thing to those called under their leadership. A radical move of God will be preceded by radical change, and I believe we are closer to that shift than ever before."

I say a hearty "Amen" to that.

CHAPTER 5

THE ONE THING MANY OF OUR CHURCHES ARE MISSING

From the 1960s to the early '80s, many people exited traditional and mainline denominational churches because their needs were not being met, and they were hungry for the deeper things of God. As a result, para-church organizations were raised up and played a key role in the training and discipleship of new converts. Bible schools were established to equip pastors and leaders. I was a part of the end of that move of God.

Many of those pastors and churches that were raised up during that time, however, have now become as structured, rigid, and set in their own agendas as the former churches they came out of.

I see a trend today that is attempting to reverse this process and avoid another mass exodus from our churches by using methods and developing programs that will either keep current members from exiting our churches or draw new people into them (that is what spurned the seeker-friendly church philosophy). Usually this is done by planning various events or offering new and exciting programs that attempt to produce a quality in the church from the outside in. And this is not the pattern of the New Testament.

The Lord gave me a word a few years ago that further magnifies this truth: *"Let the fruit grow the ministry and not the ministry grow the fruit."* He went on to use the example of the woman at the well who had an encounter with Jesus that led to an entire Samaritan city being impacted with the gospel (John 4:28-30, 39-42). The fruit of that woman's testimony produced greater ministry among the men of that city. The effectual working of God's power in her heart activated her to works of service and to testify of Jesus.

It is amazing what the effectual working of the power of God does in a human heart! The word "effectual" or "effectually" in the Greek is *"energeo"* or "energy" (1 Thes. 2:13). It is the active operation of God's power that works in them who believe. This power is what energizes God's people and activates the zeal of God in them. I believe the greatest miracle is when a heart is touched by God and set on fire and activated as the woman at the well was. Revival starts with one life, one heart that produces radical change, and, then, boom! A whole city can be touched.

How precious are those on fire for God! Those whose hearts burn with love for Jesus are the hope of the Church and the world. As previously stated, when the saints are spiritually healthy, vibrant, and full of zeal, it brings light and glory into a church and a city.

This is the pattern we see throughout the gospels and the New Testament. The key to this fruit in Jesus' own life and ministry lay in the revelation, power, and compassion He walked in as a result of His fellowship with the Father. All fruit grows and flows from within that fellowship. True Spirit-filled fellowship and fervent, heartfelt prayer is what initially makes tremendous power available (Jam. 5:16). The fruit of this power is souls being touched for God.

We cannot produce a quality in the Church from the outside in as is common in the Church world today when we start a ministry or a program, embalm it with some sort of structure, and then try to breathe spiritual life into it that will produce fruit. As already stated, the New Testament pattern is to find out where the Holy Spirit is already moving and where spiritual life is already flowing, and follow that. Then build just enough structure to facilitate that life. That way, if the operation of the Spirit of God changes, or if fruit is no longer forthcoming, there is so little structure established that things can easily be shut down or changed to facilitate a new way or a new flow of life before it becomes a form without the power. Forms have killed the life of the Church for centuries.

On the other hand, changing outward forms, structures, worship styles, adding a new mission statement, new technology, new programs, and new outreaches, changing the name of your church or ministry, although useful, are all false, unproductive ways to actually produce spiritual life. Spiritual life, health, and vitality flow from the fellowship we have with the Lord and from being continually baptized into the implications of who Jesus is to us.

Elaborate buildings, large numbers of people, and an increasing flow of cash are not necessarily a sign of spiritual life and vitality, nor does it guarantee the same. The Church did not begin with that focus, but yet somehow modern Church principles have put the emphasis on *attendance, buildings,* and *cash.* Some have called it the "ABCs" of modern church growth. But many false religions of the world have a large following, magnificent buildings, and lots of cash, too.

Although we are not opposed to any of these things in and of themselves, they are not the true indicators of spirituality. As a matter of fact, often these things serve as a sort of façade or smokescreen that hides the real problems and issues that are facing the Church in this hour. They tend to thicken our deception and fool us into a false sense of success.

The cart-before-the-horse mentality would apply here. We've been guilty of painting and decorating the cart while neglecting the sick horse — the cart being the external workings of the Church and the horse being the true spiritual condition of the people.

My younger biological brother, who is a bit of a wordsmith, came up with the following quote that illustrates the "cart before the horse" mentality that is so prevalent in the body of Christ today:

"Another meeting, another offering, another song, another convention, another banquet, another special speaker, another concert, another project, another program…and so 'church life' continues, but the changed life remains scarce. If the horse is healthy, the cart will be pulled. If the horse is unhealthy, making the cart more attractive is useless." — Roy Farias

There is a subtle, almost subconscious mentality in the Church today that places great emphasis on the outward and external appearances of Christianity. Think about this. We are trained by example to esteem appearance, presentation, professionalism, and showmanship above what is happening internally in the hearts of the people through the effectual working of the power of God. We are easily impressed by the trappings of the production of the Church and fooled by its big names and big conferences. I'm afraid there is a large gap separating the culture of the modern Western Church from the heart of God as revealed through Jesus in the gospels and through the early Church.

Sadly, in much of the Church world, the culture of the kingdom of God has been lost to the culture of hype, greed, religious politics, a Hollywood Jesus, and the professional business of the Church to such an extent that many churches resemble a political machine or a corporation more than God's culture.

God's culture begins with hearts being set free by the love and power of God and impacting their family and home — making disciples through life relationships, reaching and caring for others with the power of the gospel and the love of God. And because of the effectual working of the power of God in their lives, no one has to tell them to do the work of the ministry. The true outworking of God's power in His followers is that they become fishers of men.

In conclusion, the true disciples of Jesus are losing the taste for the shallow and superficial, and are separating themselves from those entangled in the appearance of spirituality. Many people have become disenchanted with the Church because of hurt, misuse and abuse, religious politics, theological fads, celebrity lionizing, denominational traditions, and leadership caught up in the things of the flesh.

Frankly, many of them are tired of the status quo and predictable routine. People are looking for depth in the Word and in their relationships, a free-flowing move of the Spirit, personal empowerment, and leadership that does not play political games. We need to be less concerned about the external façades and staging of modern Christianity and focus more on the spiritual lives and condition of the people.

Is the effectual working of the power of God producing mightily in them? Are they being activated from within for works of service? Are they on fire and testifying of Jesus in their spheres of influence?

CHAPTER 6

ONE BIG REASON
SPIRITUAL PEOPLE ARE LEAVING CHURCHES

"And my speech and my preaching were not with persuasive words of human wisdom, but in demonstration of the Spirit and of power, that your faith should not be in the wisdom of men but in the power of God" (1 Cor. 2:4-5).

A solid and stable friend of mine has left three churches in the last decade. She attended all of them for a number of years and then left.

In the first church, the pastor stopped having guest ministers in, and the church began to dry up from the lack of exposure to the Ephesians 4:11 ministry gifts.

In the second church, there was a small stirring of the Spirit for a while, but then the church turned to the seeker-friendly philosophy, tongues were confined to the back room, and the Holy Spirit was quenched, resulting in a lukewarm atmosphere in the church.

In the third church, again it was alright for some time, but then the leadership began to move in a different direction and incorporate modern church-growth principles and Madison Avenue tactics that grieved the Holy Spirit, and everything changed. Soon greasy doctrines slid into the church. To maintain her spiritual freedom, my friend had no choice but to leave again.

To those really seeking to encounter God, soon the fancy stage, the bright lights, the cool bands, and the video screens become just white noise to them. They want Spirit and fire.

As I said before, there was a season in Catherine Booth's life, the wife of Salvation Army founder William Booth, when she visited different churches in her area *"looking for burning words."*

Smith Wigglesworth (1859-1947) had a similar experience in which the Spirit kept telling him to come out of dead works and dead churches. He continued to move with God throughout his entire life.

One day a youth leader made an appointment with his pastor to discuss the implementation of a new program for the young people. The pastor, a deeply spiritual man, listened patiently. After the young man finished talking, the pastor responded with these words: "Mom (his wife) and I have found over the years that prayer, the Word, and moving in the gifts of the Holy Spirit have always got the job done."

Think about these examples. The same thing is happening today. When pastors and church leaders fail to follow the plan of God, some people leave because they are not being spiritually fed and fulfilled. Sometimes they cannot even articulate the reason they are leaving. They may tell you it's because of the music, or the preaching, or the youth and children's programs, but the underlying reason may be because they are not encountering God any more.

I've read articles and exit polls about the many reasons people leave their churches, but most of them are surface reasons. They make it so complex and complicated, causing more pastors and church leaders to continue re-hashing over the many ideas they could implement to increase their numbers. But is that what it's really about? The numbers? The Catholics have numbers; the Muslims have numbers; the Mormons have numbers. I would rather have 300 hungry-for-God people than 3,000 who want to be entertained.

Think about the many revivals throughout Church history. Think about the ministers God has used to pioneer some of those revivals. It was the presence and power of God in these meetings and on these ministers that drew the people. Throughout history people have always craved the supernatural. I know that the local church also caters to people's natural lives and natural needs, and cannot be run like a revival. But the people also need continual renewals and re-fillings of the Holy Spirit.

If the presence and power of God are being manifest and people still leave, what of it? Do you really want those kind of people in your church? Conversely, I know many spiritual people who are exiting their churches for lack of rain. They are not leaving due to offense or pride. They are not backsliding and leaving God, but they are leaving deadness, lightness, and superficiality. There is a cry in God's people for the waters of the Spirit and fresh new wine.

"My soul thirsts for You; my flesh longs for You in a dry and thirsty land where there is no water. So I have looked for You in the sanctuary, to see Your power and Your glory" (Ps. 63:2-3).

It is amazing what leaders can build and do without God, especially right here in America. God's stamp of approval is not on what man builds but on what He builds Himself as men cooperate with Him. Divine power can manifest only when there is an end to self-sufficiency. If you become lukewarm and stop hungering and thirsting for the Spirit, you will become a disappointment to God. I don't care how big of a building or how many people attend your church.

I love the local church. I love pastors who truly lay down their lives for the people they serve. I believe the local church to be the hope of the world. But God wants to move. He has a plan. He has a purpose. And if we don't line up with it, He has no choice but to move where He finds His people and His leaders hungering for His presence and power.

I have a pastor friend who is leading a thriving church. The adults, the youth, and the children are on fire there. He has several guest speakers and at least two revivals every year. There is an expression in his church of a diversity of the Holy Spirit's ministries and manifestations that is rare today. He is a man of love and prayer, and he listens to the Lord. By today's standards, he is unconventional in that he refuses to compromise prayer, the Word, and the moving of the Holy Spirit and implement the newest church-growth programs or the latest fads.

This church has constant revival because there is liberty in the Spirit for the Lord to do what He wants to do. This church is producing spiritual people and not clock watchers and time servers. And they are serving their community well.

Pentecostal meetings used to be called "the gate of heaven" because of all the manifestations of the Spirit and power of God they had. Testimonies of changed lives were frequent. These churches were known for tongues and power. One of the big reasons we are not seeing the power and the glory of God in many of our churches today is because we don't pray in tongues long enough for the Holy Spirit to take hold with us and give birth to these things.

Oh, people of God! Oh, ministers of the Lord! May we come to the end of our own wisdom, strength, and sufficiency!

"Not that we are sufficient of ourselves to think of anything as being from ourselves, but our sufficiency is from God" (2 Cor. 3:5).

The apostle Paul was careful to place the focus of the people he ministered to on the power of God and not on the wisdom of men. He did not want to bring attention to his own persuasive words or enticing speech. He did not want people to place their confidence on man's ability, charisma, or personality. There was nothing in his ministry that was natural. With fear and trembling, he sought to make Christ manifest everywhere he went.

Too many churches have lost the glory because their pastors and ministry leaders live too much in the natural. Get back in the Spirit. May we fall on our face and pray, and let the Spirit of God have His way.

CHAPTER 7

IT'S TIME TO UNCHURCH THE CHURCH: IS IT AN ORGANIZATION OR AN APOSTOLIC ORGANISM?

In a survey conducted in Amsterdam in the 1990s, young people were asked two questions: Are you interested in God? Are you interested in church? 100% stated they were interested in God, while 99% stated they were NOT interested in church. The pastors blamed the youth.

I believe one of the greatest barriers to effectively fulfilling the great commission could very well be the Church itself. As someone once said, "The quickest way to 'church the unchurched' may very well be to 'unchurch the Church.'"

After spending years as a missionary and more time in a stateside school of ministry that was born out of one of the recent great American revivals, I can tell you this: The Church needs to be reincarnated and redefined.

What do I mean by "unchurching the Church"?

Christianity has become too institutionalized, to where the Church is seen, at least by the outside world, as an institution built on the concept of consumerism rather than as an apostolic organism. Much of the Church is set up like a corporation, with lots of organization and structure but often with little emphasis on relationship. We must understand that the body of Christ is not primarily an organization, but rather an organism, built on relationship by the Spirit, with the Lord and with each other. Initially the early believers met in the temple, but they also met regularly from house to house and shared meals together.

The second area in which great change is needed is in our relationship to the world or to the lost. One of the principles that has caused great growth in the Yoido Full Gospel Church in Seoul, Korea (a church that numbers nearly one million people as of this writing), is the *"oikos principle."* *Oikos* is the Greek word for "household" or "house of people." Your *oikos* is that group of people with whom you relate on a regular basis. This would include your relatives, neighbors, fellow employees, those with whom you share common interests, and others with whom you may have regular contact. These people make up your personal sphere of influence.

Sometimes believers discover that there are only other believers in their *oikos*. If this is the case, then steps need to be taken to develop new circles of relationships. Throughout our early years of parenting, my wife Carolyn and I enrolled our son Daniel in sports leagues, not just so he could have fun and learn sportsmanship and teamwork but for our family to start developing relationships with the lost.

Hear the wise words of Arthur Wallis: *"There is no question that God works, often powerfully, in the old structures. But it is inevitable that those very structures put serious limitations on His working. It is all too easy for the ground gained to be lost, for the situation to revert, and for the whole process to need repairing within a short space of time. Take the 1950 Lewis Awakening. Though confined to certain Presbyterian churches in the Outer Hebrides, this was a powerful movement of the Spirit that deeply affected those communities at that time. Many found faith in Christ, and some of these are now in full-time service. But the fact remains that in less than a decade you could visit those very churches where God had worked so powerfully and never suspect that they had ever tasted revival. 'Without a change of structure it is virtually impossible to conserve the fruits of revival.'"*

When "structure" and "organization" are emphasized above relationship and the moving of the Holy Spirit, it will produce an institution that pays their workers to love and serve people. Everything then will become event-based, performance-based, and program-driven. A lack of intimacy and true covenant relationships keeps most people under-stimulated and actually serves to harden the human spirit. Authentic New Testament Christianity has as its core

John 13:35, which says, *"By this shall all men know that you are My disciples, if you have love for one another."*

When Jesus cursed the fig tree (Mk. 11:13-14), it was symbolic of the cursing of Israel's entire religious system. Today "religion" is the world's greatest curse because it does not deal with the places of the heart. That is why people can hide in churches. There is not enough Spirit, love, intimacy, accountability, and covenant.

This generation has found no relevance in the Church. They are looking for something to die for, but institutional Christianity has ripped them off. The Church needs a revolution. The Church needs an apostolic discovery of real kingdom values.

Remember, the Church did not begin with huge buildings or large organizations ruled by the appointment of men. The Church began with Jesus and the covenant relationship He modeled with the Heavenly Father and with His disciples. All relationships begin by simply being together (Acts 2:42-47). That is a part of the overall pattern that we must return to.

When this pattern is more fully realized and restored in the Church, we will produce true sons and daughters and not just programs and numbers. More impartation and not just information will be given and received.

CHAPTER 8

THE INSTITUTIONALIZATION OF CHRISTIANITY

Part I

"And seeing from afar a fig tree having leaves, He went to see if perhaps He would find something on it. When He came to it, He found nothing but leaves, for it was not the season for figs. In response Jesus said to it, 'Let no one eat fruit from you ever again.' Then Jesus went into the temple and began to drive out those who bought and sold in the temple, and overturned the tables of the money changers and the seats of those who sold doves." (Mk. 11:12-17)

Jesus cursed a fig tree just *before* He cleansed the temple and drove out all those who bought and sold there. The contrast in these parallel acts is striking. The cursing of the fig tree represented the destruction of a fruitless religious system. It served as a visual object lesson of what Jesus had come to do in the Jewish temple before He established the new covenant.

When Jesus cursed the fig tree He was cursing forms of religion that rob the heart of power. There are some concepts found in Christianity today that are robbing many of the true power of God. Allow me to briefly address these by using my limited knowledge of Church history.

When Constantine, emperor of Rome, made Christianity the official religion of the Roman Empire in the fourth century, it marked the beginning of the institutionalization of the Church. Constantine made the Church a state institution. From that point in time until the period of the dark ages (1500 AD) much of the Church died. What we've seen in the last 500 years has been the renewal, revival, and restoration of many truths and the life that had been lost in the Church age. Yet there remains a recovery and a

49

resurrection of the *effects* of the institutionalization of the Church. What do I mean by this?

There were two basic fallacies that were birthed during the institutionalization process. The first was the thought of the Church being a building. Constantine built beautiful edifices and required Christians to attend. As someone once sarcastically said: "The Church building became a theatre, the ministers the actors, and the tithes and offerings were the admittance fee." In this way, Christianity became the official religion of the Roman Empire.

Up until that time, Christians had met in homes. This change regarding Christianity and the Church meeting in large, elaborate buildings affected the mindset of multitudes of people during the Roman Empire and in future generations. The issue is not the location or venue where the Church meets, so don't get hung up there.

It doesn't matter where the Church gathers — in a big building, a small building, a house, a garage, a barn, a tent, or under a tree. The bigger issue is in possessing a New Testament mind-set that the Church is not a building but the people who are actually the temple of the living God. This may sound too simplistic, but this mindset began restricting the gospel to the four walls of a building instead of taking it into public life. It killed the evangelistic fervor of the Church. *The Church is not a building.*

We could also add, according to the above passage of scripture, that *the Church is not a business.* As soon as the Church becomes more of a business that deals only with the dollar in mind, or a social club that provides fun and entertainment for its members, or a charitable organization that is content with humanitarian projects only, it will begin to wither and die, just as the fig tree Jesus cursed. The Church, above all else, has been called to be a soul-saving organism. If the devil can institutionalize it and turn it into a powerless religious system, it will no longer serve the purposes of God.

The second fallacy, which was spawned by and developed from the

50

first, is the thought that the people are an *audience*. Beginning with the rule of Constantine and the Roman Empire, a greater distinction than God intended was made in Christianity between the clergy and the laity. This was definitely the greater tragedy during the institutionalization of the Church because it shifted the personal responsibility of the individual believer in the Church over to the institution and its officers, and the individual became a spectator instead of a participator. *The people are not an audience.*

These mindsets, or schools of thought, have robbed so many of the truth and the power of the gospel, not only centuries ago, but even today. Christianity becomes institutionalized when a building becomes more important than the people, when money becomes more important than the Spirit's workings, when attendance takes precedence over effectiveness, and organization and structure are emphasized more than relationship.

The Church is a living organism. It grows from within. You cannot produce a spiritual quality in the Church from the outside in. Changing outward forms and structures, as already stated, are false and unproductive ways to achieve quality. Spiritual quality can be produced only from the inside out.

The fig tree that Jesus cursed had leaves but no fruit. In other words, the outside looked good, but a closer inspection by Jesus exposed the tree's flaws and lack of fruit. This was the problem in the temple. It looked beautiful and unblemished on the outside but was unclean and defiled on the inside.

These mindsets can immobilize the gospel and hinder its effectiveness in the public arena. It can also create too large of a distinction between what is called the clergy and laity. Just like an unused muscle, a Christian will begin to weaken and backslide when he does not function in his gift, calling, or purpose.

What would happen if all believers would function in their place and in their God-given abilities and grace? The devil knows he cannot stop God from distributing these gifts, so he seeks to slow down or stop the joint operation of them. He hinders the freedom to exercise these gifts. And he does it through the formation of a mindset that tells the body of Christ that their ministry is insignificant compared to that of a pastor or another Ephesians 4:11 ministry gift.

Every believer is the temple of the Holy Ghost. Every believer has been given gifts to function as a vital member of the body of Christ. Every believer is set apart for the purposes of God.

CHAPTER 9

THE INSTITUTIONALIZATION OF CHRISTIANITY

Part 2

"But now we have been delivered from the Law, having died to what we were held by, so that we should serve in the newness of the Spirit and not in the oldness of the letter" (Rom. 7:6).

The Church is to reflect the life and nature of God. The quality found in any church is based on that fact alone. The more institutionalized the Church becomes, the less it reflects the life and nature of God.

Individual hearts contribute to the corporate quality of life within a church. Attempts to add quality to the Church by substituting outward forms robs the Church of the true power of God. As previously mentioned, when Jesus cursed the fig tree, He was cursing forms of religion that rob the heart of the power of God (Mk 11: 20-21).

The Law put emphasis on outward forms and restraints. Grace puts the emphasis on an inward transformation and the inward life. Law works from the outside in. Grace works from the inside out. The Law was written on tablets of stone. Grace has God's moral law written on the heart. The Law was given to spiritually dead people, but grace has been given to spirits who've been made alive. *The more Law is present in the Church, the more institutionalized it becomes.*

The institutionalization of Christianity happens when spiritually alive people are made to operate in something that was designed only for spiritually dead people. We do believers a great injustice by continually telling them what they can and cannot do, subtly teaching them that they cannot operate by the new nature. The power is in the new nature. The Law could never give us this power.

The purpose of the Law was to restrain people's flesh and sinful nature. In the Church and under grace, this becomes unnecessary. You don't need a law to restrain the new nature that has the love of God in it (Rom. 5:5). Love will restrain you if you listen to it. What is necessary is to teach and train people to yield to that new nature, which is love.

In the Old Covenant, Israel's obedience to the Law was strictly for their own benefit. They obeyed so they would be blessed and not cursed. All Israel knew was to hate their enemies, and physical death was the penalty for certain sins. They could in no way know God's love for sinners. They knew God more as a Judge and not a Father.

Do you think Jesus did what the Father told Him to do so He wouldn't be cursed? Did Jesus seek and save the lost because He wanted to be blessed and earn wages from the Father? Did Jesus forgive His enemies at the cross so He could miss hell and make heaven? No! One thousand times, no! Jesus did what He did because it was His nature.

The number-one need in the body of Christ today is the renewing of the mind so that it can come into agreement with the nature of God that dwells in every believer. Jesus fulfilled the Law by simply walking according to His nature.

How is the law present in the Church today?

1.   Under the Law, the presence of God was manifest in a temple made with human hands, a geographical location. Under grace, our bodies are now the temples of God where His presence abides. Placing an emphasis on the church as a building reinforces this aspect of the Law in people's thinking. It limits and diminishes our consciousness of God dwelling in us.

2.   Under the Law, the prophets, priests, and kings were the only ministers anointed by God for service, and the rest of Israel were dependent on them to hear from God and lead them. Under grace, all believers are kings and priests who can hear from God and are

anointed to minister in some capacity. An extreme focus on only the pastor or the other Ephesians 4:11 ministry gifts excludes or minimizes the rest of the body of Christ from participation in the service of God. Once again, this is another aspect of the Law and institutionalization of Christianity.

3. Under the Law, there were 10 commandments. Under grace, yielding to the new nature (love) fulfills all the law and commandments. Love is the new commandment Jesus has given us (Jn. 13:34).

The Church must come out from under the Law and from religion by feeding and nurturing the new nature. This will keep the Church from being institutionalized and being bound by forms that rob the heart of the power of God.

CHAPTER 10

DIVISION AND STRIFE KILL LOCAL CHURCH LIFE

I love people. I love community. I love family. The local church is all three. She consists of fathers and sons, mothers and daughters, and brothers and sisters. She is Christ's body and His sole possession that He purchased with His own precious Blood.

That last thought should make you pause and ponder the high and precious state of the Church.

I am a preacher, and I have a holy calling and a responsibility to preach the Word. According to the following verse of Scripture, preaching consists of convincing, rebuking, correcting, warning, urging, and encouraging, which are all used to show in what way people's lives are wrong.

"Herald and preach the Word! Keep your sense of urgency [stand by, be at hand and ready], whether the opportunity seems to be favorable or unfavorable. [Whether it is convenient or inconvenient, whether it is welcome or unwelcome, <u>you as preacher of the Word are to show people in what way their lives are wrong.</u>] And convince them, rebuking and correcting, warning and urging and encouraging them, being unflagging and inexhaustible in patience and teaching" (2 Tim. 4:2 – AMPC).

While fulfilling my calling and responsibilities to the Church as a preacher and a guardian of men's souls, I am also conscious of who I am preaching to. She is not only the Church, and the body of Christ, but also the radiant bride of Christ.

I am happily married. I love my wife. She is my bride. But don't pretend to love me while disrespecting and speaking evil of my bride. Don't pretend to love Jesus and disdain, divide, and damage the Church at the same time. You do not love Jesus if you treat His bride that way.

It's easy to love your wife when she is young, clean, beautiful, and sexy. It's easy to love her when she is agreeable, compatible, and conforming to your desires, and always unselfishly meeting your needs. But that's not reality, and that's not life. Your young bride will not always be young, she will not always look radiant, and she will not always please you. It takes a higher level of Christlikeness to love your spouse on days when she is not so pleasant in conduct and temperament — when her flaws are glaring and she seems so self-centered. It is the same exact way with the local church.

Griping and complaining about the church's flaws and selfishness are not going to make her any brighter or any better. If you griped and complained about my wife that way, you would wound me and hurt me. Jesus is jealous of His bride, and you wound and hurt Him the same way when you speak ill of her.

If you want the local church to be brighter and better, you've got to first see her through the blood of Jesus and His finished work on the cross. Each individual member of the church, the body of Christ, has a story of redemption. Listen to their stories. Hear their hearts that have been broken by sin, deep disappointments, and life's hardships and trials. Hug their necks that have sometimes been stiff toward God and their fellow man. Squeeze their hands. Pray for them. Love them — not only in word but also in deed.

If you are young, listen intently to those who've lived twice or three times longer than you and have served Jesus well. Honor their lifelong commitment to the Lord. They have so much to teach you. If you are older, listen to the younger ones who are living in a culture now that is five times more dysfunctional than yours was when you were their age. They need your unconditional love, unwavering patience, and unbiased acceptance. Be gracious, give them space to err, and always leave them with hope.

The local church doesn't need to be relevant, trendy, and cool for it to be effective. Those modern-day traits are so overrated — as if we can't survive without them. The Church universal has survived for 2,000 years, and her extinction is a theological impossibility. The

Church's existence really doesn't even depend on her success and maturity. Throughout the centuries, she has faced many challenges — often been immature, unfaithful, undesirable, hypocritical, manipulative, unproductive, and abusive — but God has sustained her to this hour by His mighty grace and power. In her worst times, she still remains Christ's beautiful bride. Remember that.

Instead of being a divisive force in the hand of the enemy, I want to see every member of the body of Christ be a cheerleader for the local church in this hour and add to her unity and corporate power. We are so divided over doctrine, style, ministry philosophy, etc. We find so much to disagree on and so little to agree on. If your local church is preaching and teaching the Word; if they are interested in winning lost souls and making disciples; if they are open to the moving of the Holy Spirit, then help her accomplish the commission she's been given.

I know I've included a chapter in this book on one big reason that spiritual people leave churches, but there are also many poor reasons that people leave their local churches. As I said, the local church is a family, and you just don't walk out on your family that easily and casually. The cross must be applied to our souls as we learn to love as Jesus loved.

Sometimes people leave because they are easily offended, spoiled and selfish, restless, easily unsatisfied and discontent, and critical and hypocritical. Now of course, there are legitimate reasons to leave a local church — sin and lack of integrity in leadership; heavy-handed control, poor feeding, unscriptural and unethical practices, etc., but more often than not, people leave for the aforementioned reasons.

Don't be of the generation who was fickle and caustic as the people were in the days of John the Baptist and Jesus.

"For John came neither eating nor drinking, and they say, 'He has a demon.' The Son of Man came eating and drinking, and they say, 'Look, a glutton and a winebibber, a friend of tax collectors and sinners!'" (Mt. 11:18-19).

These people were never satisfied with those God sent them, much like believers today are never satisfied with their pastor or spiritual leader. John came fasting, and they found fault. Jesus came feasting, and they found fault again. Such is the way of fickle people. If you have a legitimate complaint, be a part of the solution and not the problem. It's not all about you.

Churches and pastors are flawed and imperfect. If the heart is right, and love rules, change will be forthcoming.

Look at the Corinthians. Paul said they were carnal and contentious, and that there was envy and strife among them (1 Cor.1:11, 3:3). They had a sectarian spirit, sexual immorality was in their midst, some were eating food offered to idols, and there were theological and cultural problems. But Paul saw them through the finished work of Christ (1 Cor. 1:1-9), and with Paul's help, they worked through their many issues and problems.

We cannot be a glorious Church if we are divided. We cannot be a glorious Church unless love and unity prevail among us. Strife kills life. Whether you are young or old, be determined to be the generation that cheers loudest for the local church and adds to her unity and power. Let us be the generation whose faithfulness to Christ's Church and devotion to the saints are in direct proportion to our faithfulness and devotion to the Lord Jesus Christ.

In spite of her many flaws, let us be a part of the generation that sees the best of the church and loves her just the same. Whether the local church is thriving or struggling, let us be a contributing factor to her growth and a champion of her change.

In the end, she will shine forever and ever with the glory of her Bridegroom, so help her shine now.

CHAPTER 11

BIRTHMARKS OF A MOVE OF GOD

As soon as I walked into the meeting place, I could sense the presence of God.

We were visiting one of our spiritual sons who had planted a work in the southeast part of our country. We were only passing through. It was just Carolyn, me, and him. The atmosphere in the small building where he was holding meetings was charged with the presence and power of God. I knew him to be a man of prayer, so that did not surprise me.

Our visit encouraged him and birthed some things in him, but it also left its mark on my wife and me. I have not been able to shake it. In a day when many churches are toning down on the move of the Holy Spirit, structuring their services in such a way where it leaves no time and space for the Spirit to work, and following the latest church tactics and trends, it was refreshing to hear the testimony of a brother who is moving in the opposite direction.

There are always certain birthmarks of a real move of God in a local church or a city. Here are the ones we witnessed in the testimony of this unnamed brother and the work he is doing.

1. He is not following the money. God has led him to be high intensity on the power and glory of God and low profile on money. Of course, we are not opposed to receiving offerings, for the work of God must be supported, but in his particular case, he is not receiving conventional 10-15 minute offerings that are attached to a tithing/offering message. Instead, he leaves a basket in a corner close to the door where people can give if they choose to.

I used to think that this method of receiving offerings was a form of shame, that most people wouldn't give, and that it would cheat the people out of a blessing. But because of our day's extreme emphasis on finances and the diminishing level of trust in Christian leadership, this brother has chosen to allow people to give out of the move of God that is touching them instead of a forced agenda. It is working for him.

Money doesn't control him. He stays detached from the system of unbelief. Some men recently tried to manipulate him with a large tithe, and he sent them on their way, refusing to let them use money as a form of manipulation to control him. How refreshing that is in today's church culture!

2. He is following the glory. This work is marked by a passion for the glory of God. Many miracles, signs, and wonders are taking place. Instead of the focus being on the wealthy and those who can give, it is on the poor and those who cannot give. An example of this is seen in at least two places in Scripture: the parable of the great supper (Lk. 14:16-24) and the cleansing of the temple (Mt. 21:12-14). Instead of the traditional ministry philosophy, in which the members of the church serve the pastor and his vision, the pastor and the vision serve the people and empower them to fulfill their calling and destiny. There are rules, boundaries, and protocol, but love is the law that prevails.

In January the church did an outreach in the open air for the drug addicts, the prostitutes, the sick and diseased, and the outcasts of society in their city. Miracles were reported, and many were saved, healed, and delivered.

Periodically they began taking the gospel to the projects on Sunday afternoon after their church service. They would pray and then go out. The power of God started moving in these projects. One day about a dozen gang members and hoodlums came out, and this brother talked to them about the Lord. They wanted nothing to do with church or God. In the south, religion, man's traditions, and hypocrisy have choked the life of God from so many of its churches and embittered many people.

This brother challenged them and asked them, "If God were to come down and touch you, would you serve Him?" They answered, "Yes." Then he prayed a short prayer, and the fire of God came down on the street; they were all slain in the Spirit and fell to the ground under the power of God. Glory to God!

Every time this unnamed brother goes to the projects, some of these men now go with him. Word-of-mouth advertising is spreading quickly, people keep coming, and the Lord keeps adding to the church.

One millionaire businessman who owns the plaza (strip mall) where their facility is located has begun to tithe to the church because, since they've been there, the businesses in this plaza have been revitalized. At one time, several of the buildings were all close to foreclosure. Empty buildings are now being filled. This millionaire is not even a churchgoer and is giving to this church and work because God has touched his business.

3. Finally, the work is built on true worship and prayer. There is a love affair going on with the Lord here, and it begins at the leadership level. People are learning through precept and example to seek the face of God more than His hand. The birthing of the glory of God and the movement of Divine activity have come out of that place of true worship and prayer.

Here is something every pastor needs to know in this hour. The glory of God will take care of a thousand concerns that you have. When you satisfy the heart of God and let Him build His house on prayer, He perfects everything that concerns you. His glory touches other areas of your life and ministry, so you will never have to address them. There is a protection in the glory. Take care of His business, and He will take care of yours.

I have known for years that there is a move of the Spirit that modern-day Charismatics know nothing about, and we've got to get it back. He wants to build houses of prayer that are filled with His glory. This alone will satisfy God's heart and the heart of every man.

The works of God that will stand the test of His holy fire are gold, silver, and precious stones. Conversely, works of wood, hay, and stubble will be burned up.

My fervent admonition to you today is to go for the gold. Go for the glory. *"For unless the Lord builds the house they labor in vain that build it"* (Ps. 127:1).

Oh, ministers of the Lord, and you who bear His vessels, the Holy Spirit has been sent to help you. Pray, listen, and follow Him. This is the season in which He wants to make everything new, fresh, and alive again.

CHAPTER 12

WHY DO SO MANY PENTECOSTALS AND CHARISMATICS NOT SPEAK IN TONGUES ANY MORE?

This is an important word for those who believe in tongues. If you don't believe in them, or you believe they are not important, or that they are a gift for a chosen few, or that they've passed away and are no longer relevant for today, then this word is not for you. You can stop reading right here. But if you are under leadership who do not believe or speak or emphasize this supernatural language, you may want to consider getting out of the ditch your leadership has dug for you, especially if you are young and the better part of your life is still in front of you.

Let me say this strongly. Without tongues, there is no life and power. Period. Tongues are the connection to revelation, power, and effectiveness. When the early disciples were endued with the power of the Holy Ghost, the initial outward evidence that they had received that power was tongues. Tongues were the making of such world-renowned ministries as John G. Lake, Oral Roberts, and Kenneth E. Hagin. Someone asked Lester Sumrall how often he prayed in tongues, which generated this terse response: "When I'm not preaching." The apostle Paul told the Corinthians that he prayed in tongues "more than all of them put together," one translation says. Yet modern churches that seem to know better are departing from this sure way.

I travel to churches so I see firsthand how much of a diminishing emphasis there is on praying in tongues these days. There is a marked difference between now and just 20-30 years ago. Even in the back room in pre-service prayer, there seems to be less and less praying in tongues. And singing in tongues is even rarer and almost unheard of. More and more Christians seem to be uncomfortable and unfamiliar with this realm. This neglect is hurting the Church. This de-emphasis is diminishing her power and effectiveness. And this is exactly what the devil wants.

The use, value, and scope of tongues are so vast that it is sometimes difficult to put into words. If we are not careful, some of these things will fade away in this generation. I'm seeing it. There are certain elements of prayer, for example, that will be lost to our youth if those who are older and more experienced in these areas fail to pass them on.

There is a book in my library I often refer to. It is called, *Tongues: Beyond The Upper Room*, by the late Kenneth E. Hagin. Every believer should have that book. Every church should teach thoroughly from it. Every minister should read it regularly. There are certain men of old like Hagin and many others who were sent by God with light from heaven for their generation. The challenge with each new generation is to keep the light burning that these men brought to us from the Holy Ghost. There is a new church methodology that is making it easier to lose this light. There is a new ministry philosophy that is content to let it slip away because, according to their wisdom, it doesn't bring in the numbers or the dollars.

In the aforementioned book, there are some amazing testimonies of the miracle-working power of God that was manifested through those who strongly believed and practiced praying in tongues. One testimony is told of one Brother Boley, a missionary to West Africa. He would travel by sailboat to some primitive islands to preach the gospel to unreached tribes. One night, on his return to the mainland, a storm arose at sea. This was at the turn of the 20th century, when they did not have light or navigation equipment.

The storm was so bad that they reached a point of two choices. They could stay out at sea and be swallowed up by the turbulent waves, or they could direct the boat toward shore through the coral reef, where, in all likelihood, it would be smashed to pieces. Either way, barring a miracle, there would be loss of life to all on the boat.

Unbeknownst to Brother Boley, one of his helpers back at the mission station on the mainland had a burden to pray that night. Not knowing the situation or even quite what she was sensing, she prayed in tongues for about two hours. Then the burden lifted, and she had a note of victory that the answer had come. The Old Pentecostals called this "praying through" — something so few Christians know anything about today. This is one of the elements of prayer modern Pentecostals and Charismatics are losing.

Kenneth E. Hagin heard Brother Boley in person share this testimony, or else I would've had a hard time believing it myself. Around the same time that the burden of prayer lifted off this woman, the boat took off in the air like an airplane and sailed over the dangerous reef and landed in the harbor, where the waters were calm and peaceful. There was much rejoicing, and not a life was lost.

Why are we not seeing and hearing more testimonies like this today? It's simple — because we are not praying very much in other tongues. The next wave of God's Spirit is dependent on the prayers of God's people. Ministers who know and have experience in these areas need to teach more on the Holy Ghost and prayer, and then demonstrate some of it to the people. The Lord told Kenneth E. Hagin that the greatest move of God would come through the combination of the solid foundation of the Word that's been built over the last few decades and the power of the Holy Ghost that will be manifested as we learn to enter into this deeper realm of prayer.

Here is a powerful quote from Hagin in the book I referred to above:

"Oh yes, we've seen the power of the Holy Ghost in a limited fashion, but a wave is coming that will bring His power on a higher level and in a far greater measure than we have ever seen before. I can see that wave out yonder in the deep waters. It's coming!

"Don't stay on the old wave of yesterday's move of the Spirit. Swim out to the deep waters of the Spirit realm by praying in the Holy Ghost, and get on the next wave of God's purposes for this hour. Then keep on praying so you can ride that new wave as it builds in divine power and

glory.

"I'm convinced the wave that is coming will be twice as high as the healing wave, the Charismatic wave, or the faith wave. In fact, it will be twice as high as all of them put together! I believe it is going to be the wave that sweeps us right on into the shores of the glory world!"

It is surely not a time to back off from the Holy Ghost and praying in tongues. Instead, it is time to double up and triple up on praying in other tongues so that we can see our mighty God display His great power in this time of gross darkness on the earth.

CHAPTER 13

THE IGNORANCE ON THE SUBJECT OF TONGUES IS MIND-BOGGLING

I've included a few of the many public comments from an article I wrote that was published by a large magazine, to expose the blatant ignorance there still exists in the Church and among professing believers today on the subject of tongues.

Here are some remarks from that article:

I began the article by mentioning three pioneers of the faith who said that tongues was the making of their ministries, but that mention was met with great irreverence by one individual.

1. *"John G. Lake was a known fake healer who was also a financial huckster. His inability to heal led to the death of a girl named Hannah Anderson and almost crippled another girl who had a fractured thigh.*

"Oral Roberts: His shameful attempts to get rich off of his "ministry" are well known. Anyone remember him saying God would kill him if people didn't send him 8 million dollars?

"Kenneth Hagin: He spread the Word of Faith heresy and plagiarized Kenyon.

"If these people are examples of what comes from speaking in tongues, I think I'll stick with regular English, thanks."

What can I say? Such disregard and disdain for some of God's choice servants stop people from receiving the light from God that these men carried to the Church. It is difficult for me to understand such professing Christians. This is eerily equivalent to the Pharisees and religious leaders calling Jesus a devil and attributing His works to demons (Mt. 12:24).

Here are the rest of his comments:

"Tongues? You think it is the be all and end all. But really, it's just laziness. God doesn't want mindless drones — otherwise he wouldn't have given us free will. I mean, really — do you honestly believe that God (Who knows everything) would require some random person to babble things they don't understand in order to save someone? Next time you pray — don't take the easy way out. Actually talk to your Father."

Wow! Just half a scripture refutes this person's ignorant statements.

"For he who speaks in an unknown tongue does not speak to men but to God…" (1 Cor. 14:2a).

The commentator continues: *"Paul said in the Bible that tongues were one of the least of the gifts of the Holy Spirit. Yes, I believe some have that gift, but does one have to have it to be more spiritual than those that do not have it, or does one have to have that gift to be saved? No, the Bible does not say that."*

This person missed the entire point of the article. He chose to fixate his thoughts and words on traditions he had been brainwashed with instead of rightly dividing the word of God.

This person makes three errors in his brief statements. First of all, the devotional exercise of praying privately in other tongues is never called a gift in Scripture. The gift is the Holy Spirit, also called the promise of the Father, or the baptism in the Holy Spirit, which is available to every person in every generation (Acts 2:39). The word "gift" is never associated with tongues until 1 Cor. 12, when it is called "divers[e] kinds of tongues." It is the public-ministry gift of tongues that requires interpretation for the edification of the hearers.

Secondly, the baptism of the Holy Spirit with the evidence of speaking in other tongues is for personal edification, which should add to our spirituality in the sense that it makes us more effective witnesses and pray-ers. How many Christians can you name who do not speak in tongues but move in the gifts of the Holy Spirit? Not many. Why? Because they've not received the baptism in the Holy Spirit that Jesus sent for service.

Thirdly, the gift of the Holy Spirit with tongues is separate from salvation. They are two distinct experiences, so we should not confuse the two. Jesus spoke of salvation as a *"well of water"* (Jn. 4:14), and the baptism in the Holy Spirit as *"rivers of living water"* (Jn. 7:38). Simple. If these individuals would stop trying to interpret Scripture through their traditionally colored glasses and listen and learn, instead of speak and teach, they would actually be enlightened. The problem with many of them is they've been religiously brainwashed instead of New Testament taught.

This next person makes the same mistake while adding another statement that increases his confusion.

2. *"Speaking in tongues is not the only gift of the Holy Spirit. There are many others that are just as important, if not more. I would think there would be a practical application of speaking in another language for guests who may not understand the local language quite as well."*

Once again, tongues, as in "divers[e] kinds of tongues," is a gift, but he is confusing this gift with the simple gift of the baptism in the Spirit with tongues for personal edification. This is the most common error among those who do not believe that this experience is for every Christian.

Secondly, he confuses the sign at Pentecost, when the tongues they spoke were actual languages the nations at Jerusalem understood, with the private use of tongues for personal edification. There are different purposes and uses of tongues. Actually, there are at least four uses/purposes of tongues.

a. They are for personal edification (1 Cor. 14:4).

b. They are one of the gifts of the Holy Spirit for public use with interpretation (1 Cor. 14:27).

c. They are a means of prayer and intercession (Rom. 8:26-28).

71

d. They are a sign to the unbeliever when understood in their own language (Acts 2:7-12).

Here's another one of his comments: *"Paul said tongues was the least, not the first, yet some people think tongues is the first and a must-have to be holy. I don't agree, but it is one of the gifts, not a have-to-have to be right with God and holy."*

This individual is another who confuses the simple gift of tongues for edification with the public gift that needs an interpretation. But he goes a step further and confuses tongues with holiness. Tongues are not a prerequisite for holiness. The fruit of holiness is the fruit of the Spirit, and every born-again believer has the Spirit within them so that they can produce the fruit of holiness in their lives.

On the other hand, the Corinthians were baptized in the Holy Spirit and enriched in the gifts (1 Cor. 1:4-7), but Paul said they were yet carnal because there was strife and divisions among them (1 Cor. 3:1-3). This proves that the baptism in the Holy Spirit is not primarily to produce holiness in our lives but power (Acts 1:8). Of course, God's best is to have both fruit and power.

3. *"Tongues are not to be turned on and off by people but given utterance by the Holy Spirit."*

This individual seems to imply that speaking in tongues is controlled by the Holy Spirit. This may be partly true (because the human vessel must cooperate with the Spirit of God) for the public gift of "divers[e] tongues" that requires an interpretation, but it is not true for the private use of tongues, which a believer receives when he is baptized in the Holy Spirit. The former is as the Spirit wills (1 Cor. 12:11), and the other is as we will.

Paul said he could pray or even sing in tongues at will (1 Cor. 14:15).

This next person seems to be quite sure of his position and even acts as the expert teacher who wants to teach his pupil a Bible lesson.

4. *"Bert, your article on tongues is based on cheerleading without a*

shred of authentication. You rely on stories instead of the Word. I pray in tongues. I have for 40 years. When it wants to come up, I go with it."

We've already covered this. He believes you need to wait for a spirit of ecstasy before you can speak in tongues.

"But I do not ascribe miracles to tongues that are not found in Scripture. When you make tongues a cure-all, you are way out of bounds, encouraging us to live in la-la land."

A thorough study of Romans 8:26-28 in the Greek will shed much light on how praying with groanings, which includes tongues, is indeed connected to miracles of healing and salvation and even spiritual growth and gives birth to such. Time and space will not permit me to write further on this.

The person continues:

"Consider this: for all the praying in tongues that Pentecostals and Charismatics (PCs) have done over the eons, it has not stopped America from sliding into the muck of immorality and godlessness. America as a nation has gone to hell in a hand-basket while PCs prayed in tongues, believing it is a cure-all for all of our problems. The Church has seen a great falling away from the Word while we prayed in tongues. You must stick with Scripture, Bert, when you speak of the benefits of tongues, or you're teaching error."

I concur with the reverse of what this person is stating — that the very reason America is in bad shape is because the Church has done too much mental praying in English and not enough spiritual praying in other tongues.

"Please consider this: when you make tongues the answer for everything, you become part of why so many leave tongues alone. Tongues were given to spread the gospel to those speaking foreign languages. They were meant to awe those who heard it, as they knew those speaking didn't know their language. It was a sign given by God to them to persuade

73

them to believe in Jesus, but PCs have made it a way of getting people healed. That's nonsense."

The nonsense here is that this Christian takes the preposterous position that tongues are for preaching in other languages, but we have already seen that this is only one use or purpose of tongues and is subject to the will of the Spirit. When understood by the hearers, which happens only occasionally, it is a sign to them of the reality of God. The main use of tongues is for personal edification and prayer.

"You have no scripture for that. You're teaching us to live by what we think, not by the Word. The only reason I pray in tongues is because it sometimes wants to come up, if I don't know how to pray, so I let it fly, but since I cannot know what I am saying, I cannot put faith in my tongues to fix the problems at hand. It is the prayer of faith in Jesus that saves the sick, and tongues cannot be prayed in faith, believing for healing, as you know not what you say. Stick with scripture, Bert, so those who read you will not live by illusions and fantasies."

What else can be said? This individual is all muddled up and tangled up in seeing tongues from only one angle. I never said that tongues will fix all our problems, but it will sure fix many of our problems because you will be dealing with life's issues from a place of personal edification and revelation. Speaking in tongues does not give you faith for everything, but it stimulates the faith you already have from the Word (Jude 19-20). My advice to this commentator is that he needs to learn the Scriptures himself.

Here's one final comment from yet another individual.

5. *"Tongues were given as a ministry tool but we made it a private prayer language and changed it from a true language to praying in English syllables, calling it a language of the heart. Where do we find scripture for that?"*

The same error keeps being repeated. Can you see that? Several of these believers are not distinguishing the difference between the private and public use of tongues. It is a ministry tool, in a sense, and it is also a private prayer language.

"For he who speaks in a tongue does not speak to men but to God, for no one understands him; however, in the spirit he speaks mysteries" (1 Cor. 14:2).

These many comments reveal again to me that spiritual ministers need to teach more on the topic of tongues, so that believers can exercise their faith in utilizing their personal use of it. There is too much confusion in this area that needs the light of the Scriptures to bring clarity and understanding.

CHAPTER 14

OPERATION OF THE FLESH OR THE SPIRIT?

"That which is born of the flesh is flesh; and that which is born of the Spirit is spirit" (John 3:6).

"Are ye so foolish? Having begun in the Spirit, are ye now made perfect by the flesh?" (Gal. 3:3)

The Lord has given me a holy zeal for the manifestation of the full spectrum of all things pertaining to the Holy Ghost. I see everything a failure without the workings of God's Spirit. The programs, the projects, the props, and all the ministry professionalism is futile without the demonstration of God's Spirit and power.

There are two ditches. One is hype, sensationalism, and entertainment. The other is formality, deadness, and ritualism. We must find that delicate balance between unwholesome fanaticism/wildfire and no fire at all.

I see two primary groups that have evolved and emerged in the body of Christ today. I see an older group who came out of dead formalism decades ago. They exited traditional and mainline denominational churches because their needs were not being met, and they were hungry for the deeper things of God. As a result, para-church organizations were raised up and played a key role in the training and discipleship of new converts. Bible schools were established to equip pastors and leaders. As we've stated before, many of those pastors and churches that were raised up during that time, however, have now become as structured, rigid, and set in their own agendas as the former churches they came out of. That's one group.

I have never seen so many so-called full gospel churches and denominations who have left the way of the Spirit and resorted to the methods, machinery, and traditions of men to try to get the job done.

The second group is a new generation of churches and pastors who do not know the real move of the Spirit but utilize substitutes such as contemporary forms of worship, the arts, visualization, and imagination in an attempt to demonstrate the Spirit. All of these things are in the category of "prophetic arts." These substitutes result in a barren church void of the real Spirit and are vulnerable to demonstrations of the flesh and even doctrines of devils.

These two large groups do not even include the segment of churches today who are totally ignorant of the operation, administration, and manifestation of the Holy Spirit in His gifts and ministries (1 Cor. 12:4-11, 28) (Eph. 4:11). I thank God for the remnant of those Word-and-Spirit churches who are still carrying the torch and moving strong in the Word and in the authentic ministry of the Holy Spirit. They are a treasure in this hour.

There are quiet churches who resemble graveyards, and there are noisy churches who are just as dead. It is not being quiet or being loud that confirms the presence and power of God. It is that indescribable something called *the anointing*.

Who can describe, much less produce, the freshness of a morning when orient pearls abound on every blade of grass? Such is the essence of the precious anointing of the Holy Spirit. We may know it and discern it, yet we are unable to tell others what it is. Its counterfeit is worse than worthless, for no one can ever manufacture it, though they continue to try. But the true anointing of the Spirit is priceless and such a necessity for edification, impartation, and a true equipping of God's people.

Honestly, most Pentecostal and Charismatic Christians today cannot tell the difference between the operation of the flesh and the operation of the Spirit. Most can't tell the difference between prophesying in the flesh and prophesying in the Spirit, giving a message in tongues without the anointing and with the anointing, dancing in the flesh or dancing in the Spirit, running and shouting in the flesh versus doing it in the Spirit, singing with the anointing and singing without it, etc.

You see, when things are done in the Spirit, there is something like a sweet-smelling fragrance that pervades the atmosphere. Pastors and ministers have got to learn the difference so they can teach their people. We've got either too much dead formality or too much fleshly showboating in the Church today. Still some, who claim to know the difference, have difficulty discerning between brass and gold. It takes a trained eye and ear to know it. What do I mean by the difference between brass and gold?

In the Old Testament, Solomon built the temple/house of the Lord and overlaid the oracle, the altar, and the entire house with gold. He also made all the vessels, treasures, and utensils of the temple out of pure gold (1 Kings 6 and 7). Then the king of Egypt came against Jerusalem and removed the treasures from the house of the Lord, and King Rehoboam later replaced them with brass (2 Chron. 12:9-10). This is what Christians have done in the Church. They have brought the brass of the world into the Church and used it as a substitute for pure gold. They've brought the music, the clapping, and the singing and dancing of the world into the Church.

God wants to help us minister the Spirit. If we will truly sanctify ourselves and just learn to praise and worship the Lord in the Spirit, we would experience deeper levels of the presence and power of God in our midst.

WILL THE REAL HOLY GHOST PLEASE STAND UP?

"And my speech and my preaching were not with persuasive words of human wisdom, but in demonstration of the Spirit and of power, that your faith should not be in the wisdom of men but in the power of God" (1 Cor. 2:4-5).

"And the things that you have heard from me among many witnesses, commit these to faithful men who will be able to teach others also" (2 Tim. 2:2).

There are real demonstrations of the Spirit, and then there are also demonstrations of the flesh. As I stated, the body of Christ has got to learn the difference. There will be a move of the Spirit that will be

79

lost to this present generation if it is not passed on through precept and example by those who know something about it.

One time a young believer prophesied: "Don't be scared, my children, but if you are scared, that's okay, because I get scared sometimes Myself."

Now that prophecy is easy to judge, isn't it? It would be funny if it weren't so pathetic.

Here is an excerpt of another prophecy that someone once gave: "I have no other church like this church. And I've put you on a pedestal for the world to see how great I've made you."

That one is also easy to judge. A true prophecy will never exalt a church or a man like that to where they think so highly of themselves. And not all prophecy is from heaven to earth, or "thus saith the Lord" utterances. Much of prophecy is from earth to heaven.

For example, speaking or singing in psalms, hymns, and spiritual songs by the inspiration of the Holy Ghost is prophecy. This is something every believer should be doing in their personal prayer life. Also, preaching by the inspiration of the Holy Ghost has an element of prophecy in it. I've preached nearly entire messages that were by the spirit of prophecy.

There is more error in the utterance gifts ("divers[e] tongues," interpretation of tongues, and prophecy) than in the other gifts because we initiate those gifts. They are supposed to be initiated by the unction of the Holy Ghost, but many do not know the difference between the anointing and their own emotions or mind.

Many of today's prophecies draw attention to the greatness of a man. We don't see that in the New Testament. Go through the book of Acts and tell me where you find that. True prophecy will edify, exhort, and comfort us and glorify God, not glorify man. There is no reverence for God in a word that magnifies and draws attention to man.

Lack of true reverence for God is one of the problems in the

Church today. There is a lightness and a casualness in many of our gatherings. People come in late. They move around or leave casually during the meeting. There have been times over the years when I've been preaching or prophesying under the anointing of the Spirit and people get distracted or restless and start moving around. Even as a former Catholic, I had more reverence for God than that.

A "hip-hip hooray," clap-happy attitude is dissipating the presence and power of God from our midst.

It's difficult sometimes to impart that understanding to people. If you correct them strongly, many times they will become quiet and unresponsive to the Spirit when He does move. The old-time Pentecostals knew something about the deeper move of the Spirit. This new generation of Pentecostals and modern Charismatics know almost nothing about the real depth of the move of God's Spirit. Instead of cooperating with the Spirit of God, people often hinder Him. We need to be sensitive.

Years ago, one Sunday, I was visiting my parents' home church, and while sitting in the congregation, the Spirit of God came on me to dance. I don't usually dance unless I'm really prompted to by the Spirit, especially as a visitor somewhere. The seats were close together, so I stepped out in the aisle and began to dance. A person sitting behind me got up and tapped me on my shoulder and told me he couldn't see the words of the song on the screen because I was blocking his view. As soon as he did that, the Spirit of God just flew away like a bird, and I lost the unction to dance. If that person had been sensitive, he would've been dancing himself.

We don't dance just to put on something. Neither do we dance just to keep time with the music, or because we like the beat. That's dancing in the flesh. Dancing in the Spirit brings God's presence and refreshing to a congregation. It is not only the person dancing who gets blessed; those in the meeting who are in the Spirit also get blessed. There's a heavenly fragrance that goes out over the whole crowd sometimes. When there's liberty like that in a meeting, great things can happen, and there is often an increase of angelic activity.

Several years ago when I was preaching in another nation, there was an outbreak of joy and liberty in the Holy Ghost, and people were healed without anyone touching them or praying for them. There was a young demon-possessed man outside the meeting venue on the streets who was arrested by the power of God and couldn't move. He was stuck to the ground. Eventually he came loose, and some ushers brought him into the meeting. There he was set free, born again, and Spirit filled in those days of meetings.

When there is too much formality and ritualism in a meeting, it kills the liberty of the Spirit and brings a heaviness.

In some of our meetings, my wife will often take the microphone and begin praying or singing in the Spirit. As she does, often the atmosphere becomes impregnated with the presence of God. At times, I can't start the meeting the way I intended to. Preliminaries are scratched out as we move together in the Spirit in another direction. A greater liberty comes, and it changes the entire meeting. Every praise and worship leader ought to move in that operation to prepare the way for the Spirit of God and His gifts.

Praise and worship in the Spirit will give birth to manifestations, and the opposite is also true. Manifestations of the Spirit, like tongues and interpretation, a prophecy, a revelation, or a healing will also give birth to high praise and worship in the Spirit. Often dancing and rejoicing in the Spirit breaks out. The aftereffects of meetings like that bring believers closer to the Lord and can carry them for weeks, or until they learn to get filled up themselves.

I've been in gatherings when people have just danced to put on something, or danced to the music. As I've said, that's just fleshly dancing. Now, music helps, but you don't even need music to dance in the Spirit. There are now churches that conduct dance classes to teach people how to dance. You can't teach people to dance in the Spirit. Dancing is a result of being filled with the Spirit.

There is also laughter in the Spirit. Many refer to it as holy laughter. Some don't understand it, or they make mockery of it because they've never been in the Spirit. At times, I laugh in my own personal prayer time. I've had belly laughs and begged the Lord to stop because my stomach was hurting. People are often healed by laughing and set free from bondage or oppression. You see, because people are negative by nature, they tend to criticize what they don't understand or have never experienced. That is how it is with the things of the Spirit.

Even reputable men in the body of Christ have criticized the move of the Spirit because of all the excesses and extremes they've seen. Some have even denied the entire thing and call the Pentecostal/Charismatic movement a fraud. And some of these are leading men who oversee entire denominations and congregations of people. How sad and how grievous it is to deceive and divide the body of Christ like that!

One of the drawbacks I see an increase in today is people doing things without the anointing. Recently I went to a minister's prayer meeting, and one young minister prophesied over me for about five minutes. None of it was right. I did not bear witness to any of his words. He went on about how he saw this and he saw that, and it was just all his imagination. He substituted imagination for true revelation. Of course, we can all miss it like this from time to time, but it shouldn't be because we are trying to put on something. A person can close his eyes or keep them open and see anything he wants. Many claim to have visions, but many times they are mind visions, not spiritual visions. A person can visualize anything they imagine. And yet I absolutely believe in visions and revelation and seeing and knowing things by the Spirit of God.

The plan of God in the New Testament is for every believer to be filled with the Spirit and to maintain that infilling. The older and more experienced ministers have got to teach, demonstrate, and lead people into these things. When they don't, then people will try to substitute other things for it. There will be fakery, hype, and superficiality as people try and fill that void and barren-ness, or they will continue on in their traditions and unbelief and have deadness and dryness.

Oh, but when the real move of the Spirit of God is in manifestation in our midst and we flow with Him, that river will get deeper and wider, and we will enjoy His presence and the needs of the people will be met.

Praise God forevermore!

CHAPTER 15

PROPHETS OR FORTUNE TELLERS? IT'S ABOUT TIME WE LEARN THE DIFFERENCE

There is a growing false prophetic movement in this country that must be addressed and confronted. Unsound doctrine and counterfeit prophecy are diluting the manifestation of God's presence and power and polluting the landscape of Christianity today.

"Son of man, prophesy against the false prophets of Israel who are inventing their own prophecies. Say to them, 'Listen to the word of the LORD'" (Ez. 13:2 — NLT).

"I have not sent these prophets, yet they run around claiming to speak for me. I have given them no message, yet they go on prophesying. If they had stood before me and listened to me they would have spoken my words, and they would have turned my people from their evil ways and deeds" (Jer. 23:21-22 — NLT).

"Beloved, do not believe every spirit, but test the spirits, whether they are of God; because many false prophets have gone out into the world" (1 Jn. 4:1).

While I do believe in the valid ministry of the prophet and have been a personal beneficiary of such ministry, I have also been increasingly alarmed at what passes for true prophetic ministry today.

Here is a typical word of what passes for prophecy today.

"I have called you to a high calling, says the Lord, and I will lift you up to a place of great glory, and money will no longer be a problem for you, for I will move on people's hearts who will contribute to your wealth. You will no longer minister in small circles, but soon television will open up new arenas to you, and your ministry will be greatly sought after. In that day, you will know the favor of your Daddy God, and He will increase you more and more."

Have you heard of a similar word in today's marketplace of Christianity? A word like that is clearly carnal, man exalting, and flesh pleasing. It feeds pride, covetousness, and the inordinate affection for recognition and influence that are in people's hearts. It is the basest and most subtle form of idolatry.

Examples of such prophecies are numerous in this day, and sadly, the norm. Usually they will address one of three areas in a person's life: Ministry, money, or marriage. They will speak to a person's discontentment and need for recognition and promotion, or their strong desire to be blessed and happy through possessing the riches and comforts of this life.

Now compare that prophecy to this one.

"I am going to prepare you for the coming days by a hard path that will cause many to cry out continually unto Me. For when the going is easy, men do not seek Me, but rejoice in a temporary blessing. And when that blessing is removed, they so often turn this way and that way but do not come to Me. I am showing you these things in order that you may seek Me continually and with great diligence. As you seek Me, I will open up truths to you that you have not seen before, and these very truths will be such that will enable you to stand in these last days. As you are persecuted, reviled, and rejected by your brethren, then you will turn unto Me with all your heart and seek Me for that spiritual life that you need."

This one speaks of the trials that are part of this Christian life and grants hope of the sustaining spiritual life of the Lord as we seek Him.

The former example speaks of ease, comfort, and the presumed blessing of great ministry and financial prosperity. Due to the abundance of counterfeit prophecies in this day, you hardly hear the latter kind any more.

I wouldn't pay a nickel for that first word. There is nothing in it.

It is not that the Lord is opposed to His people being blessed and happy, but such prophecies are dangerous when they feed impure motives already resident in the heart. The true prophetic should direct people's hearts toward God and not our own selfish and soulish desires.

Do you know how many desperate single women have been prophesied to about a future husband who never came? Many of them grew bitter with time, and their wounds led them into severe depression. Evil spirits attached to such words of divination hang around them for years.

I know of young men who went into the ministry because of a prophecy, and it wasted years of their lives and nearly ruined them. Others abruptly changed the course of their previous plans to pursue a prophetic word that pointed them in a different direction. These types of prophecies are like fortune telling that cause great damage to the body of Christ and pollute the land.

Here are three basic differences between the real and the counterfeit prophecies that will help you discern:

1. The counterfeit is man centered and brings excessive attention to the recognition and greatness of man. The real reveals the true heart of God and directs our hearts toward Him.

2. The counterfeit feeds the idolatry in our hearts, which is covetousness (Col. 3:5), and feeds our carnal desires for selfish gain and a satisfaction that's unattached to God's will and heart for us. Real prophecy will offer hope and encouragement during hardship but often with an exhortation toward humility and praise, or a warning to guard against the selfish motives and the lack of character in our hearts.

3. The counterfeit will drift from the pure written Word with a mixture of flesh/soul, with some spirit added in. But the real will contain within it a solid Scriptural foundation that acts as a sword dividing the flesh/soul from the spirit, or our own desires from God's will.

The root of most prophetic abuses is the covetousness in the hearts of both the giver and recipient of such. False prophets can easily get over into a performance mode that even familiar spirits will accommodate. Familiar spirits know things about people and possess knowledge of their past and present. Some prophecies can also be accurate because those prophets may have a genuine gift but are operating with wrong motives.

Be very careful.

People's love for power will cause them to pursue it more than purity, thus defiling their own hearts. False prophets are like fortune tellers that lead people into deeper idolatry.

We must understand that if there is idolatry already in someone's heart, it will only be strengthened by the dainty prophecies that appeal to their flesh and to their pride. That was the problem in Israel when the majority of the prophets were speaking peace and prosperity and victory, but the Lord saw the idolatry and wanted His people to turn from it. Any prophecy that feeds our carnal and fleshly motives needs to be questioned. Deception will work in us when we receive and embrace words that are not from God.

A true prophet carries an anointing to turn the hearts of the people from sin, self, and idolatry toward the Lord. And frankly, that is what the Church needs most in this hour.

Therein lies a great key that will help you tremendously in your discernment. What is happening to your heart when the prophecy is being given? Is it strongly being drawn to the Lord, or does it merely make you feel special, superior, and even elite? Does it draw you to the Lord or to the person giving you the prophecy? Does it feed your humility or your pride?

The bottom line is that much of what passes as prophetic ministry today, although done in the Lord's Name, is not done by His Spirit or according to His heart.

In this 21st-century quagmire of idolatrous worship and ministry, may we truly be among the remnant that will be taught of the Lord.

CHAPTER 16

THE DEMONSTRATION OF THE SPIRIT AND POWER OF GOD: ARE YOU AN AQUARIUM KEEPER OR AN OCEAN SWIMMER?

"And my speech and my preaching were not with persuasive words of human wisdom, but in demonstration of the Spirit and of power, that your faith should not be in the wisdom of men but in the power of God" (1 Cor. 2:4-5).

I had a dream recently of a pastor who was worshipping the Lord in a service, but all around him there were distractions, people were not paying attention, and hardly anyone was focusing on the service. Then the Spirit of the Lord showed me that there was no expectation in the service because the pastor had built a low spiritual ceiling. This is the present-hour situation in many churches today, and this is an important word for ministers and saints.

The Word alone is not enough to equip the saints. The demonstration of the Spirit and power of God in the gifts and through His ministers is necessary, too. Why else would God set them in the Church?

When the Spirit is released and the power of God is demonstrated, it ignites the saints to do the work of the ministry. This is when a body of believers is the strongest. The demonstration of God's Spirit and power even ignites the service gifts and what is commonly called the ministry of helps (1 Cor. 12:28). A leader won't have to constantly ask the people to serve or arduously recruit volunteers. The joy of serving and moving with God is ignited through the demonstrations. The people are always willing in the day of God's power (Ps. 110:3).

Sarah is an example. When we ministered in the Spirit at her church, she received an impartation. She was ignited with expectation and excitement. She was touched, filled, and something changed in her. This type of thing consistently happens in the hearts of the saints who are exposed to real Spirit-empowered ministry.

Even as far back as the beginning of the Church age, the seven men chosen to wait on tables were to be men filled with the Spirit (Acts 6:3). The apostles' quality decision to stick with their unwavering devotion to prayer and the Word kept them in a place of always ministering the Spirit. This is where the focus of ministers needs to be.

Not only will it help ignite the saints when the demonstration of the Spirit is on, but it helps the preacher and teacher and God's ministers, for they, too, are ignited in their spirits. God's workings affect their utterances, and there is a greater kick and "umph" in their ministry; their words are freighted with the Spirit's authority.

When pastors make the choice to back away or turn off the move of the Holy Spirit, it diminishes the power of God to fill every heart, and it opens the door to other things to where people have to be entertained, because their hearts are not satisfied and fulfilled in the Lord.

Years ago, during a series of Holy Ghost meetings, the senior pastor of a large Charismatic church shut off the lights and closed the meetings down on a guest minister. There was joy being manifested in the meetings with unusual manifestations, and many of the saints were getting filled and liberated. All kinds of spiritual activity happens when God starts moving like this. To abruptly and irreverently shut down a meeting where God is moving, even when there is some extravagance, is to slap God in the face.

What followed shortly after in this church was tragic, as marriages went sour, divorce and adultery became rampant, heretical doctrines surfaced, and many people backslid. This is what happens when pastors stop or hinder the move of the Holy Spirit or refuse to allow Him to move. It is better to put up with a little extravagance than to quash or quench the liberty of the Spirit.

I call this "the aquarium effect." Studies have shown that if you

90

put a certain species of a large fish in a small aquarium, it will not grow beyond the size of the tank. When a pastor puts too many limitations on a service or on the church, it not only quenches the Holy Spirit, but it also limits the expression of the kingdom and the growth and freedom of the people and who they are. There must be an expression of extravagance, or you will kill the anointing through formality. You might say: "What if chaos breaks out? After all, Paul told the Corinthians to do things decently and in order."

Here is the simple answer to that concern. Paul laid out some guidelines and protocol for their gatherings (1 Cor. 14). What we must ask ourselves is this: Is it Holy Ghost chaos or is it fleshly chaos? Does it minister edification or confusion? The Spirit's wisdom is always liberty with limitations.

In a kingdom mindset, each one has something (1 Cor. 14:26); the Ephesian 4:11 ministries are free to demonstrate the Spirit and power of God, and each joint makes its supply (Eph. 4:16). When everything has to be sifted through a pastoral controlling mindset, people will reach a spiritual ceiling. Pastors who are concerned with only their vision and how they want things done will produce an aquarium effect. Those who are truly following God's plan are kingdom builders and moving in an ocean with no confinement or ceiling. Their pulpits and ministries are submitted to the Spirit of the Lord, and they recognize that their responsibility is more to oversee, direct, and interpret the move of God, rather than control or quench it.

I am thinking of two pastor friends right now who fall on the godly side of this example. In their churches, there is much liberty, with some limitations. Actually, knowing both of them well, I would venture to say that, if they had to err, they would err on the side of liberty rather than on the side of having too many limitations that would quench the joy and liberty of the Holy Spirit. Their churches buzz with excitement and the joyful activity of the saints. As a result, more increase keeps being given to them.

There is an awakening to the Spirit of God in pastors right now, especially upon those who are listening and paying attention to the Lord. They know something is missing. They know they made a wrong turn somewhere. They are about to retrace their steps and move back into the will and plan of God for their lives, ministries, and churches.

Pastors of local churches who sincerely desire the plan of God will have soulical/emotional ties removed from their make-up, and they won't be able to go back to familiar settings. It will be more difficult, however, for denominational pastors or those in controlled settings to wade out into the waters of the move of God. Once a man comes under a system of humanly designed agendas, where the wisdom of man has preeminence and man's traditions are esteemed higher than God's plan, there will be attachments and restrictions in that organization.

Do you want to be an aquarium keeper or an ocean swimmer? The Brownsville revival and its legacy were brought to a halt for this very reason. The president of the Bible school, where I was also a part of the faculty, was an ocean swimmer, but the denomination tried to make him an aquarium keeper. The whole thing unraveled when man put his restrictions on it. When the reputation of man becomes more important than the glory of God, there will always be a spiritual abortion. Any minister who comes under a man or an organization that has many restrictions will be hindered if their calling is to be an ocean swimmer instead of an aquarium keeper.

The expectation of spiritually hungry people whose leadership has constructed low spiritual ceilings will collide with the raw power of God and the demonstration of the Spirit they know is available. There is coming an exodus of hungry saints from churches that have restricted and hindered the demonstration of the Spirit and the power of God.

It's time to get out of the aquarium and into the ocean now, before the rude awakening comes. It's time to wade out into the deeper waters of God's ocean and start swimming in the Holy Ghost. You'll be glad you did.

CHAPTER 17

THE VARYING MOODS OF THE HOLY GHOST

As a minister I've been privileged over the years to be in all kinds of meetings. There are always participators and spectators who attend — believers, curiosity-motivated seekers, thrill chasers, skeptics, and, at times, even mockers, scoffers, and scorners.

I would say that the meetings most people have a difficult time receiving, embracing, and participating in are the Holy Ghost meetings that exude much joy, laughter, dancing, and wild demonstrations. Concerning these type of meetings, I've heard the following criticisms from various Christians:

• We need to reverence God and not carry on with such foolishness.

• These are fleshly manifestations and a bunch of emotionalism.

• This is not scriptural. Show me that in the Word!

• If it's God, there will be change in the people, but if their lives don't change, then it's not God.

These types of critical comments are a failure in Christians to understand the multi-faceted nature and personality of God. He is not always serious.

The Holy Ghost has many moods. Sometimes the Father plays with His children, and other times He lets His children play. In Spirit-filled meetings, people will often exhibit a drunkenness and wild, playful behavior that cause some to be skeptical and label such behavior irreverent. But true irreverence would be not to enter into the mood that the Holy Ghost is manifesting at the moment. Irreverence is to be serious when it's time to play. Many do not know this playful aspect of the Father. As long as it's done in the Spirit, it will always bring edification and blessing to the people.

God said He would pour out His Spirit on all flesh beginning in Acts 2. Often when this happens, there are wild manifestations. People are filled with the Holy Ghost and joy, singing, and laughter erupt. People run, dance, and shout. In the presence of the Lord, there is fullness of joy (Ps. 16:11). The caution is not to manufacture it in the flesh but simply to cooperate and flow with the Spirit.

Have you ever seen a drunk man? How does he act? Often they display some very wild, unusual, and funny behavior, don't they? It's the same with being filled or drunk in the Spirit minus the hangover.

"Be not drunk with wine wherein is excess but filled (or be drunk) with the Holy Spirit" (Eph. 5:18).

And yes, people do change and are transformed in God's presence. But soon they will be sober again and will need to fill up once more. I've seen people healed, delivered, and set free from all kinds of oppression and bondages in such joy-filled meetings. The best is when you can take that blessing home with you and have it in your own, individual prayer life.

Many Christians know only one side of God or only one mood and stream of the Holy Ghost. Denominations and different streams of faith are usually familiar only with their particular brand or stream of how God manifests Himself within their group. And frankly, in many places, He is hardly ever allowed to manifest Himself at all.

As I stated, God is multi-faceted in His character and personality, and the Holy Ghost has many moods. We've already mentioned the joy and hilarity by which the Lord manifests Himself at times. Here are other moods and atmospheres by which God manifests:

1. The fear of the Lord — This is what happened in Acts 5 when Ananias and Sapphira were struck dead for lying to the Holy Ghost. I've been in meetings where the Spirit of the fear of the Lord was manifest, and you could hear a pin drop. Everyone was quiet and reverent or with their face in their hands, weeping. Some would be prostrate on the floor. No one wanted to talk because the atmosphere was so impregnated with a holy fear.

2. The miracle atmosphere — This atmosphere is in operation when God flexes His muscles and manifests His power to heal all kinds of sicknesses and diseases. People are delivered of various ailments, the lame walk, the blind see, and demons are cast out, or they just leave. The people witnessed this in Samaria through the ministry of Philip (Acts 8). And by the way, there was great joy in that city.

3. The sweetness of the Lord — This is an anointing that touches people deep in their emotions. It manifests in healing for broken hearts and people who are desperate and hurting. It is the Lord moving in His kindness and compassion. We see this continually in the ministry of Jesus. It was also usually accompanied with physical healings and miracles.

When the Holy Ghost manifests Himself in these various ways, just flow with it and participate. Don't stand back and criticize it because you don't understand it or are not familiar with it.

Judge everything by the anointing and the presence of God that is there. Are people being healed and delivered? Are they being filled with the Spirit? Are they being blessed and helped? If so, then rejoice in what the Lord is doing. Thank God He is not boring.

Get acquainted with your Father. Get to know the multi-faceted personality and moods of the Holy Ghost and the manifold wisdom of God. Receive all the Lord has for you. Go outside your own camp if you have to.

Be glad and rejoice in the goodness of God.

CHAPTER 18

HOW TO MOVE UP IN THE SPIRIT

Someone asked the elder Kenneth E. Hagin, when he was at the end of his years, if he had any regrets. He responded by saying he wish he had taught more on the importance of speaking and singing in psalms, hymns, and spiritual songs (Eph. 5:19) (Col. 3:16).

Why is this so important? Why is this so necessary?

God's plan under the new covenant is for His people to be continually filled with the Spirit. Speaking or singing divinely inspired utterances, whether it be in tongues or with your own understanding, is the primary way we stay filled. These psalms, hymns, and songs are not rehearsed or recited from a songbook, but they are given by the Spirit. The general pattern throughout the Scriptures is that, when believers were filled with the Holy Spirit, they spoke either in tongues and/or with their own understanding in prophecy and praise.

At Pentecost, in Acts 2:1-4, they were filled with the Holy Spirit and BEGAN TO SPEAK.

At Cornelius's house, in Acts 10:44-46, the Holy Spirit was poured out on the Gentiles for *"they heard them SPEAK with tongues and magnify God."*

At Ephesus, in Acts 19:1-6, when Paul laid hands on believers, *"the Holy Ghost came on them and they SPAKE with tongues and prophesied."*

Notice Eph. 5:18-19: *"And do not be drunk with wine wherein is excess; but be filled with the Spirit, SPEAKING to yourselves in psalms, hymns, and spiritual songs, singing and making melody in your heart to the Lord."*

These Ephesians were believers who had already received the initial infilling of the Holy Ghost, and Paul is reminding them to maintain that infilling. The Greek reads literally, *"be being filled with the Spirit"* implying continual action. Paul is encouraging these Christians to maintain a continual experience of being filled with the Spirit by speaking forth in supernatural utterances. This is one form of New Testament worship. You can get so filled with the Spirit that you are drunk. What a blessing!

The way that these utterances come is usually after a time of praying in tongues and fine-tuning your spirit. For me, I will usually sense a phrase or a word or two that arises in my spirit. Then, as I sense the unction of the Holy Spirit, I will speak or sometimes sing out the rest of it by faith. Beyond the initial phrase or a couple of words, I do not know what I am going to say. Without the anointing of the Holy Spirit, I would stumble and be lost. It takes faith. When I speak what I have by faith, the rest of it comes by the spirit of prophecy.

Here are some examples of Spirit-inspired psalms from my own life:

FULL AND FREE — *(When you stay full, you stay free)*

And so the Lord has chosen this foolish way to be the delight of those who know Him,

To uplift His children and to fill them to overflowing until the very blessing of Heaven,

Clean and clear, holy and right, be showered upon them.

And so what you've known as a trickle of living water shall become a cup,

And what you've known as a cup shall become a bucket-full,

And what you've known as a bucket-full shall become a stream,

Yea, even streams of living water flowing inside thee,

To reside in thee and make thee fat and flourishing,

Until those streams even become like mighty rushing rivers

Flowing strong to make you full and free,

Just the way the Lord of glory intended it to be.

For He is glory and His kingdom is glorious,

And so ought not His own children be full of His own likeness and glory?

Ought not His children be full of His own beauty and holiness?

And ought not they be free from every weight and sin?

Glowing without and full within,

Blossoming as a rose in the desert,

Ripe with life as God knows it,

Yea, this is the way to be full,

Yea, this is the way to be free,

Speaking and singing to yourself

With psalms, hymns, and spiritual songs,

Making melody in your heart to the Lord.

Here is another psalm:

CLEAN AND CLEAR — (When you stay clean, you stay clear)

A clean and clear blessing of God is available to anyone born of Him,

This blessing is a surge of power that comes down from the Father above,

From whom comes every good and perfect gift.

Yea, this is the gift with a lift,

It is sent to build up and edify your inner man, to strengthen and to charge,

And make you glad in the Lord,

To enrich your spiritual life, and to comfort you and encourage you in times of trial and test,

To bless you with the joy of the Lord, and lay thine own plans to rest.

Yea, a clean and clear blessing is available to anyone born of God,

It's up to you to make it flow,

Stir it up and make it go.

The Bible says to stir up the gift of God that is within you (2 Tim. 1:6). As you begin to pray in tongues at length, you will sense words rising up within you. Speak out what you have, and you'll step over into the spirit of prophecy. You can also sing in tongues and sing out the interpretation if you'd like. As you exercise yourself in these things, you will be edified and built up in the Spirit, and you'll begin to move up to a higher level spiritually.

ANOINTED WITH FRESH OIL

The psalmist of old said, *"But my horn You have exalted like a wild ox; I have been anointed with fresh oil"* (Ps. 92:10).

I love how the Amplified reads: *"But my horn [my emblem of strength and power] You have exalted like that of a wild ox; I am anointed with fresh oil [for Your service]."*

The apostle Paul encouraged early believers to stay filled with the Spirit in these Scriptures we've already referred to.

"Wherefore be ye not unwise, but understanding what the will of the Lord is. And be not drunk with wine, wherein is excess; but be filled with the Spirit; speaking to yourselves in psalms and hymns and spiritual songs, singing and making melody in your heart to the Lord" (Eph. 5:17-19).

100

The wise person understands the will of the Lord. Wise believers know that the will of the Lord is to be full of the Spirit as a drunk man would be full of wine. This is God's highest purpose in the New Testament. When one is full of the Spirit, his heart moves in prayer; he is moved for lost souls; he is holy and consecrated. He's full of whatever God is full of. He's full of love; he's full of praise and thanksgiving; he's full of power.

These Ephesian believers were already initially filled or baptized with the Holy Spirit. The baptism of the Holy Spirit was part of the essentials of first-century Christian life. Unlike today, it was not an option but a vital necessity in every single church. Since then, the devil has diluted this essential and clouded it with so much controversy. The Church as a whole will never fully do the works of Jesus until they are filled with the Spirit and maintain that infilling.

The Holy Spirit is the life of the Church. Being filled with the Spirit and staying filled with the Spirit produces a fresh anointing. Without the free-flowing move of the Holy Spirit, the Church dries up and becomes full of dead formalism.

Here's an interesting verse:

"Dead flies cause the ointment of the apothecary to send forth a stinking savour" (Ec. 10:1).

Here is the Farias translation: "Dead formalism kills the anointing and stinks up the place."

There's too much dead formalism in the Church today, and it produces a stinking savor instead of a fresh anointing. Even so-called "full-gospel churches" can lose their fresh oil if they don't stay full of the Spirit. To be anointed with fresh oil means the oil can become old and stale, which requires a replenishing. It means the psalmist was once anointed with oil, but, now, it's not fresh any more (Ps. 92:10b).

Maintaining a continual infilling of the Holy Ghost and a fresh anointing is the pattern for living in God's plan under the new covenant. It is a top priority in the kingdom of God. And it starts with each individual believer receiving the initial baptism of the Holy Spirit, speaking forth inspired utterances in tongues and in their understanding, and then maintaining that infilling by continuing on in these things.

The baptism of the Holy Ghost with the initial evidence of speaking in other tongues should not be a one-time experience but a continual stream that should never dry up in one's life. We cannot afford to live on one-time experiences of the past.

D.L. Moody once said, *"People living on past experiences are living on stale manna."*

There is fresh oil available to you and me every single day if we will stay long enough in the presence of God — until we are filled.

Here is a twin scripture to Eph. 5:18-19:

"Let the word of Christ dwell in you richly in all wisdom; teaching and admonishing one another in psalms and hymns and spiritual songs, singing with grace in your hearts to the Lord" (Col. 3:16).

Back in the early days of Christianity, they did not have a written Bible yet. The word of Christ was either the word the apostles passed down to the Christians and/or the word that the Holy Ghost would give them at the moment. Here Paul is encouraging these believers to allow the Word to dwell in them richly. In other words, he is telling them to be full of the Word. Being full of the Word and full of the Spirit will produce a fresh anointing in one's life.

Notice also that this is not just something that is done privately in your own, individual life but that it can also be done publicly, as a means of teaching and admonishing "one another."

The Lord is endeavoring to get His Church to understand these things so that His power and glory will be in greater manifestation in this final hour.

We're going to move into a place of spirituality we haven't been before, but the way you're going to get there is to learn to speak or sing in psalms, hymns, and spiritual songs, and commune with God in your spirit. Praying or speaking in tongues helps you get over into that realm.

I've also found, through experience, that often light, revelation, and direction will come after a time of speaking in psalms, hymns, and spiritual songs, or after extended seasons of praying in other tongues.

GOD'S PLAN TODAY IS FOR ALL BELIEVERS TO BE FILLED WITH THE SPIRIT

The apostle Paul told the Ephesian believers to not be drunk with wine but to be filled with the Spirit — to be drunk with the Spirit instead (Eph. 5:18). You can be so filled with the Holy Spirit that you get drunk.

Smith Wigglesworth came to a place in his life where he could get drunk any time he wanted to, and, then, when he was around sinners who lacked understanding in these things, he could immediately get sober. What a life! In his younger years, though, he was cantankerous and a backslider. There was even a season where he would frequent the bars and drink. Then he got baptized in the Holy Ghost and received his prayer language, and everything changed for him.

When Paul told the Ephesian believers to be filled with the Spirit, he was not telling them to be baptized with the Holy Ghost with the evidence of speaking in other tongues. They had already been initially baptized (Acts 19:1-6). Paul is now encouraging them to maintain a constant experience of staying filled with the Spirit. He is encouraging them to keep drinking. A person who drinks wine or other liquor usually needs more than one drink to get drunk.

The will of the Lord is for His children to keep drinking of His Spirit. Some have just learned to drink better than others. All can learn and grow in maintaining the Spirit-filled life. As I've said, the Spirit-filled life is maintained through speaking or singing Spirit-inspired utterances, whether it be in tongues or with your understanding.

One day, on a visit home from college, my son and I went for a walk together, and I revisited with him the importance of staying filled with the Holy Ghost. Then we prayed in tongues quietly as we walked in a semi-secluded area, and I took him into speaking in psalms, hymns, and spiritual songs. Because he'd been exposed to these things as a child and teenager, he was keen spiritually, so he got it. On Sunday, in a house meeting, he sang out a spiritual song publicly. It blessed the few who were there and brought the meeting to another level spiritually.

In that same meeting, the Lord ministered to a brother who was oppressed and instructed him to sing the Word and make melody in his heart, instead of just reading it. This instruction was so he could stir up his joy and resist the oppression he was under. For some people, that may be a good place to start. The Scriptures also tell us to make a joyful noise unto the Lord (Ps. 100:1). That alone could also help stir up others. But the best way to tap into this Spirit-filled life is to use your prayer language of new tongues to begin to fine-tune your spirit to these things.

God's New Testament plan and pattern is for believers to keep being filled with the Spirit.

"And when they had prayed, the place was shaken where they were assembled together; and they were all filled with the Holy Ghost, and they spoke the word of God with boldness" (Acts 4:31).

These early Christians were already baptized in the Holy Spirit in Acts 2, but notice that, here, they were filled again in a prayer meeting. When they prayed together, the power of God was manifested and shook the place where they were gathered. Christians sometimes get excited when they shake or fall under the power of God, but wait until the house or the building shakes!

I believe as the coming of the Lord draws nearer, these kinds of miracle manifestations will come into fullness. God wants to restore the fullness of His gifts, His power, and the signs and wonders that leave people in awe of God. And it's going to happen through a

Spirit-filled people.

MOVING UP AND MOVING ON INTO THE SUPERNATURAL

Here are some great prophecies spoken by the late Kenneth E. Hagin that address the Spirit-filled life:

1

"And it shall come to pass that men shall know and they shall see and they shall understand, but by so doing they must tune their spirits, tune into heaven, tune into the glory world, tune into the power and the ability and the revelation of the Father God. And so it is that then you shall do the works that He intended you should do. And the plan of God shall be consummated in these last days and the glory of God will be revealed unto man. The Church shall be enhanced, the saints shall be gladdened, sinners shall come to the Lord, the sick shall be healed, and the blessings shall be disbursed on every hand, and the glory of the Lord shall be seen by man."

2

"Seeing, seeing, seeing into the Spirit realm and then knowing that there are not only angels but there are demons and evil spirits all around about carrying on the work of their master, but angels are waiting for you to tell them what to do. The demons responding to their master Satan and doing what he tells them to do, but you and we are the body of Christ. Jesus is only the Head and the Head cannot do anything without the body. Why doesn't Jesus rebuke the devil? Why does Jesus let the devil do these things? He can't do anything about it. Your head cannot do a single thing without your body. All the prerogatives of the Head are carried out by the body. He's waiting for you."

3

"Two worlds, two worlds, yes, there are two worlds — there's the world of the natural and there's the world of the spiritual — there's the world of the natural and there's the world of the supernatural. Man lives

in both worlds. It is just one step out of the natural into the supernatural, so step out of the natural into the supernatural, and begin to speak with your mouth that which the Spirit reveals unto you and you'll find out that He'll guide you into all truth, that He'll show you things to come, that He'll minister to your spirit and buoy you up in faith, so that you'll face the enemy and will not relent, but will take your place and put him on the run. For it is written, 'Resist the devil and he will flee from you.' If you'll resist him he'll always flee. Well, someone said, 'I resisted him and he didn't go.' Well, then the Scripture is a lie, but no, God's Word is truth and truth prevails. Amen.

So walk in the light of the Word and dwell in the realm of the supernatural. Walk in the light of the revealed Word and further revelation will come, and you'll see and you'll know that the blessings of God are yours; and that which you need, to you shall be shown, and that which you see shall come to pass. And so ere the manifestation of the Spirit in the greater and most glorious manifestations of working of miracles, of special faith, of gifts of healing, ere and before they shall ever come to pass, you will find you'll have to enter in first to this realm; for this is the entrance and the door into this realm of utterance and then the spirit of seeing, and the spirit of knowing shall be made manifest."

Praise God! Let us no longer draw back, but let us enter in.

CHAPTER 19

TONGUES AND INTERPRETATION:
THE CROWN JEWELS OF THE NEW TESTAMENT

When many Christians speak of tongues, they call it a gift. But the word "gift" is not associated with tongues until the 12th chapter of Corinthians, when Paul begins his discourse on the gifts and ministries of the Holy Spirit. We must differentiate between the private and the public use of tongues.

If you want to get technical about it, there is no such thing in the Bible as the gift of tongues. Now don't misunderstand me: Generally speaking, everything God gives is a gift, but specifically, no.

The initial physical evidence of receiving the baptism of the Holy Spirit is speaking in tongues. These tongues are attached to the baptism of the Holy Spirit and are for our devotional use. They belong to every born-again Christian, but the tongues is not the gift. The Holy Spirit is the gift (Acts 2:38-39).

The gift of tongues is first mentioned in 1 Cor. 12:10 and is called "divers[e] kinds of tongues."

There is much ignorance in the church world today concerning the topic and private use of devotional tongues and even more ignorance concerning the public gift and use of "divers[e] kinds of tongues." And yet if you think about it, "divers[e] kinds of tongues," along with interpretation of tongues, are the only two gifts that were not operative in the Old Testament.

The prophets and those God anointed in the Old Testament moved in every other gift except those two. God manifested Himself in what has been termed as the revelation gifts (word of knowledge, word of wisdom, and discerning of spirits), in the power gifts (working of miracles, gifts of healing, and special faith), and in prophecy. You will find references and examples of these gifts being in manifestation throughout the entire Old Testament. But you will not find one reference or example of "divers[e] tongues" and interpretation of tongues being manifest. What does this tell us?

It tells us that Jesus reserved these twin gifts for His glorious Church. They are the signature gifts of the New Testament. They are the crown jewels of the Bride of Christ. And yet many consider them to be the lesser gifts, when actually these two gifts should be manifested more frequently than any other. Why don't we see more manifestations of these two gifts? Once again, it is because there has been much ignorance concerning them, and God does not want us ignorant (1 Cor. 12:1).

The widespread ignorance is also the reason Paul brought so much correction in the use of these gifts (1 Cor. 14). But many pastors and preachers stay away from this chapter. Most don't understand it.

In our travels, as the Lord leads us, we've been exhorting churches, by precept and example, on the proper use of these gifts. Often we will give people an opportunity to exercise giving a message in tongues. I am convinced that this is the easiest gift for a Christian to exercise as long as you have an interpreter present.

Here is a marvelous testimony of one dear sister who gave a message in tongues for the first time in her Christian life.

"Recently a couple that I know invited people to come and hear Bert minister.

"I really felt the presence of the Lord during worship. To be honest, I didn't want it to stop — it was so wonderful (Carolyn was leading worship).

"Bert started ministering, and he started talking on a topic that hasn't been talked about for a long time, and that is speaking in tongues and having the interpretation of that tongue.

"After he was finished, he asked for volunteers who have never had this gift used in their lives before. My hand shot right up — almost

108

involuntarily. In times past, I would have never done anything like that because the fear of looking stupid or being embarrassed has always held me back — but not that night. My desire for more of the Lord overruled any fears.

"Three of us came forward, and I stood there in front of the people who were there and had no fear whatsoever. I was even willing to fail if that's what happened.

"Bert handled us so well. He encouraged us, and I felt very comfortable with him when it was my turn to speak. I just stood there with my hands held out, waiting for something, and then — all of a sudden — I felt the Holy Spirit on me. Bert said, 'There it is,' and I started speaking in tongues. I could tell it was different from my devotional tongue. When I stopped, Bert had the interpretation of it. That was the first time in all of my 44 years of being a Christian that I experienced that gift.

"So, two wonderful things happened to me that night — I was delivered from fear and received a beautiful gift.

"I pray that this gift that was given to us by the Lord would come back into the church. I pray for my church — maybe the Lord could even start with me." S. M.

Isn't that a wonderful testimony? It is time to train God's people in these things by precept and example. It is time for local church pastors and leaders to take their rightful place in the ministry of the Holy Spirit and for the Church to move strongly in this direction.

TONGUES AND INTERPRETATION: DECENTLY AND IN ORDER

Many Christians have a good strong devotional tongue and are candidates for giving messages in tongues during a public service. What I mean by a good, strong tongue is that there is some depth and diversity in it. If your devotional tongue consists of only a few of the same syllables repeated over and over again, then you are not yet a candidate to give a public message in tongues. Work on cultivating your heavenly prayer language first.

Recent statistics reveal that only approximately 15% of all Spirit-baptized believers pray in other tongues on a regular basis. Some are just negligent, while others do not have much fluency and a flow of liberty in their tongues. As a general rule, the more you use it, the larger and more expansive your prayer language becomes.

The second element in giving public messages in tongues is that you must have an interpreter present. You might ask, "How would you know if there is an interpreter present?" By example. If the pastor/minister or the leader of the meeting has not set the pattern and example for these twin gifts to be exercised in your gatherings, then, more than likely, it will not happen. You've heard it said — everything starts with leadership.

Have you ever been in a meeting and someone in the congregation belts out a loud tongue — and no one interprets it? It could be in a large meeting or a smaller one. The reason there is no interpreter is because one has not been assigned. And what usually happens is that there is a long un-edifying lull, and the leader might ask if there is someone who can give the interpretation for the tongue. Or, someone may attempt to give an interpretation of it, but perhaps it is inaccurate or from someone who is a stranger to the church community. The Bible says to know the leaders who labor among you (1 Thes. 5:12). Another possibility may be that the tongue never gets interpreted. When any of these things happen, there is usually confusion.

The most comfortable, accurate, and secure interpretation that people will have confidence in will usually come from a recognized leader or a seasoned minister or, at the least, someone who's been trained and has some experience. Furthermore, there has to be some kind of protocol given to people so that they will know the boundaries of what, when, and how they are to give what they receive from the Spirit of God.

For example, one pastor has open-mic night, and he puts a handkerchief over the microphone when the meeting is closed to any participation from those gathered or when it is not appropriate to do so. Another pastor will have people raise their hand or step to the front when they have something from the Spirit to share with the congregation. Establishing some sort of protocol is necessary to avoid disorder, confusion, and chaos like they had in Corinth before Paul brought correction (1 Cor. 14).

We don't want disorder, chaos, and confusion. We want decency and order. We want liberty, but with limitations. Although liberty without limitations will gender maximum participation, it will usually not produce maximum edification. On the other hand, limitations without much liberty will stifle and quench the Spirit. The balance we are after is liberty with limitations.

"If any man speak in an unknown tongue, let it be by two, or at the most by three, and that by course; and let one interpret" (1 Cor. 14:27).

The full participation of these gifts works best under seasoned leadership and in smaller churches or home groups. In larger churches, the operation of these gifts should mainly be demonstrated by seasoned ministers or those who've been proven and assigned to such. In other words, they have been given liberty to exercise such gifts in a public service.

Again, all these points are moot if there is no interpreter. If every pastor would ask the Lord for interpretation or, better yet, to be an interpreter of public meetings, I am confident the Lord would grant it. Why would the Lord want to keep the leader in the dark about these things? If he is the pastor or the leader, then he should know the flow and direction of any service and have the ability to interpret messages in tongues.

Therein lies the problem, though. As one of my highly respected spiritual fathers used to always say, "Most pastors wouldn't recognize the Holy Ghost if he walked in with a red suit and a red hat on." I don't say that to be disrespectful. For years, I was not schooled in these things either; thus the necessity for more ministerial training.

We've trained people privately to conduct or move in 1 Cor. 14:26-type meetings. These types of meetings are mainly conducted only when believers are present. Training people privately is a real safe way to begin. I've led teams on mission trips and conducted early-morning training sessions with them. In about an hour or two, I'd have several of them giving a message in tongues for the first time in their lives or moving in prophecy. Now if I was pastoring a church, I would probably have a few more training sessions with certain, select candidates before giving them liberty to exercise these gifts in larger public meetings. When I say public, I mean when mostly believers are present.

So here are the elements that produce decency, order, and liberty in such believers' meetings and that will cause maximum edification:

1. Training by precept and example. Believers must receive teaching and instruction with demonstration in these gifts.

2. There must be certain protocols to establish boundaries as to what, when, and how to exercise these gifts.

3. These gifts must be demonstrated by those who've been trained and proven in private, smaller sessions before allowing them to minister in larger settings.

4. There must be an interpreter present.

5. All pastors who lead their congregations should be able to interpret messages in tongues and the flow of public meetings. If they ask the Lord, I'm sure He will grant them that ability.

HOW I GOT STARTED AND MORE HELPFUL GEMS

There I sat at the kitchen table of our home after enjoying a nice dinner with special friends. Then one of my spiritual fathers, Dr. Ron Smith, spontaneously, as he would often do, turned to one of our sisters and told her that she was to give a tongue and I was to interpret. This happened twice.

Privately, afterwards, I told Papa Ron, as we affectionately called him, that I did not think I had done a good job of interpreting our sister's tongue. His response to my concern was a revelation to me. He told me that the onus is not on the interpreter but on the person giving the message in tongues.

In other words, the person giving the tongue must move in an anointing and depth of diversity in word and gesture that a good interpreter will be able to pick up. The tongue should trigger revelation and authority in the interpreter.

I'm not sure Papa Ron knew that this was the first time our sister had given a public message in tongues. I had compassion on her, but this is how Papa Ron operated. He was a master at drawing the gifts out in other people, not just in public services, but sometimes also during informal gatherings. You had to be on your toes, spiritually.

You might ask, "How would one know they have a message in tongues?" Through the anointing, example, and experience of it. There's a quickening in you. You know that the Holy Spirit wants to interject an utterance, and you step forth in faith and give it. You sense He wants to punctuate a sermon or a conversation with His higher thoughts and revelation.

For example, often when I am preaching in a public service, my wife will stand up and give a tongue in the middle of my preaching. She has permission to do that, and in churches where liberty is given, she will have an extra microphone just in case she has something from the Spirit.

In a believers' gathering, it is rather obvious that we are there to share what the Lord has given us for the edification of everyone present. So we should expect these things.

"How is it then, brethren? Whenever you come together, each of you has a psalm, has a teaching, has a tongue, has a revelation, has an interpretation. Let all things be done for edification" (1 Cor. 14:26).

In my New King James Bible, this verse places the word

"revelation" in between "tongue" and "interpretation." I believe that is intentional and not incidental. There is a revelation in the tongue that a good interpreter will draw out.

In 30 years of ministry, I've been privileged to see varied uses of the twin gifts of tongues and interpretation, and move in some of them personally and with my wife. We have seen these gifts manifested not only to congregations but also to individuals. They bring revelation, edification, exhortation, and comfort. I've also witnessed the use of these gifts to minister physical healing to people. They are tremendous in their diversity.

There is much confusion concerning tongues and interpretation today because people have not been rightly taught by precept and example. Not only have people confused the private and public use of tongues, but they've confused their different purposes as well. We mentioned these purposes earlier, but let's go over them again.

For example, in Acts 2, we see that tongues was manifested in the streets of Jerusalem as a sign to the unbelievers gathered there from many nations (v. 5-12). The newly spiritually baptized Galileans were speaking in other languages never learned that were understood by the other nationalities that were there. How wonderful! And yet, that is only one of their purposes — *a sign to the unbelievers.*

A second purpose of tongues — and the most common — is that it is simply *a means of personal edification* where you build yourself up on your most holy faith (1 Cor. 14:4) (Jude 20). You can speak or sing in tongues, and even pray that you would interpret with your understanding, so that you mind would be fruitful (1 Cor. 14:13-15).

A third purpose is a means of *praying the mysteries of God* (1 Cor. 14:2) or things we know not to pray for as we ought (Rom. 8:26). It is especially to be used in *making intercession* for people and for situations. This kind of praying gives birth to the real purposes of God.

And the fourth and final purpose of tongues ("divers[e]") is for the public ministry of *interpretation,* as we've been sharing.

Here is another testimony from a woman in one of our meetings who was given her first opportunity to give a message in tongues:

"The biggest life-changing event for me was when you and Papa Ron were at our church for a leadership-equipping meeting, and Papa Ron had us stand up one at a time and speak in tongues. Once we did, you or Pastor James interpreted what we said. It was so amazing to me that I was actually praising and exalting God! I think first and foremost, we as believers need to believe that, when we are speaking in tongues, we are actually prophesying, edifying ourselves, or praising God, etc. Many people wonder if they are really saying anything at all or just repeating something they have heard others say. Hearing the interpretation of my utterance in the spirit brought me to a whole new level of confidence and boldness. I thank God for that meeting with you and Papa Ron." M. M.

Praise the Lord! Sometimes all people need is an opportunity to exercise a gift like this to grow in their confidence and boldness as a Christian.

I trust that this instruction is providing clarity concerning this important topic that has been so neglected, misunderstood, and abused in today's churches.

CHAPTER 20

RESTORING THE WORD AND THE SPIRIT TO PRESENT AND FUTURE GENERATIONS

We have many self-appointed prophets, mystics, and sensationalists in the church world today. They seem to always be looking for something new — a new word; a new experience; a new phenomenon. And so, those who listen to them and follow them are easily fooled. They don't have a strong foundation in the Word of God and are not familiar with the anointing that teaches them and leads them into all truth. They don't know how to build on revealed truth and blend the old and the new together.

A few years ago, one church member arrogantly said to me, "Hagin is dead (speaking of the late Kenneth E. Hagin), and the word of faith is dead. God is doing a new thing."

I walked away shaking my head, appalled at the ignorance of this person.

First of all, the word of faith (Rom. 10:8) is the Word of God, and that will never die.

Secondly, when the Lord restores a truth to the body of Christ, you don't throw that truth away once another truth is revealed. That's unwise.

What many call the "word of faith" in its purest form was just a restoration of the integrity of the Word of God and exercising our faith in it. Were there extremes in this move and teaching? There will always be extremes.

There will always be dirty bath water, but you don't throw out the baby with it.

Thirdly, without faith we can't please God (Heb. 11:6). So to ignorantly say that the "word of faith" is dead is like saying that faith is dead, or worse yet, the Word of God is dead.

The truth is that many have forsaken the strong foundational teaching that our forefathers laid down for us.

Martin Luther was instrumental in restoring the truth of salvation by faith and not by works. Puritan preachers like John Wesley and later Charles Finney helped to establish the Church in holiness and sanctification. At the turn of the 19th century, the baptism of the Holy Spirit was restored through outpourings such as the Azusa Street and Welch revivals. In the 1940s and 50s, there was a great, widespread healing revival that restored the reality and ministry of healings and miracles to a greater degree. Each truth was to be laid on top of the other.

During the 1960s and into the '80s, there was a wave of strong teaching where tremendous truths on faith, prayer, and the authority of the believer, among many others, were touted from our nation's pulpits.

Understanding on the gifts of the Holy Spirit and the ministry gifts increased. In my opinion we reached a peak in the 1980s, but then some things were aborted or miscarried.

In the 1990s, we witnessed the Toronto Blessing and the Brownsville Revival. There was holy laughter and holy fire. Both revivals or outpourings were controversial with manifestations of the Holy Spirit that many doubted. But always, the wise ones would learn to throw away the dirty bath water and keep the baby. God was showing us that He wanted us to let His Spirit move.

We should be building on each of these truths. Instead we have churches yet today who are still living in Martin Luther's day with salvation-only messages. We have electricity today that lights every home, but they are still living in the day of candlelight. We have Pentecostals who have left their heritage of the power of the Holy Ghost. And thus we have too many coming up in the young

118

generation today who are weak in the Word and know so little of the Spirit and His power and workings.

If we don't pass these truths and this light on to the next generation, these things will die. There must be a mingling of the generations.

TWO DREAMS

My wife Carolyn was given two dreams. One of the dreams was of two rooms separated by dividers with teachers and students in them. The dividers were then opened as the teachers and students began mingling. Then the dividers were shut again.

A seasoned minister who represented the older guard was obeying God in transferring responsibilities to the younger. He let go and said he had some other things God wanted him to do.

But there were challenges in the transfer. There was an unbending in the mature and a lack of revelation knowledge in the young ones. The Lord said that the Holy Spirit is the equalizer. There must be a transference of the Spirit from one generation to the next, for it is the Spirit and not the traditions of men that brings life.

The mature refused to bend to new songs, new colors, new decorations etc., but the young thought all they needed was the flash and the glitter, while neglecting the power of the Spirit.

The Lord said that the young generation has no business telling the older generation to keep the Holy Spirit out. Rather, they who are of the younger generation must learn the Spirit and transfer it on to yet the next generation coming up after them.

Each generation needs to keep imparting spiritual things to their children and making sure they are exposed to the workings of the Holy Spirit.

SECOND DREAM

The second dream was of another elder who was turning things over to the younger generation, but they were given more to

119

entertainment and didn't have a proper foundation. In the dream the younger people were trying to fit things into a house without a proper foundation. A table wouldn't fit into the house, so the young people pushed it to try to make it fit, and the house started to fall.

The Lord showed us that our own son was not called to a traditional ministry. He has to reach his generation through a different way because they won't listen to the traditional way. Although the commission remains the same, it will be a different operation. What do I mean by that? The Word and the Spirit remain the same, but the method or vehicle of how it is carried will often change in every generation. The wineskins that carry the wine are ever changing. From tents in the 1940s and '50s to the large, open-air crusades, from storefront buildings to large, elaborate structures, from the brick-and-mortar temples to houses, the Word and the Spirit must be carried and transferred to each new generation.

Again, the Word is our sure foundation, but the Holy Spirit supplies the life. The Holy Spirit is the One who gives life to the Word. He makes everything new, fresh, and alive again. Relationships and marriages are affected by the joy and liberty of Holy Spirit meetings. He will change atmospheres in homes as people are impacted by His life and power. Things come into order in people's hearts and lives. The Person and work of the Holy Spirit must be esteemed.

The apostle Paul wrote one entire chapter to bring correction to the confusion and the disorder that was happening in the Corinthian church during their believers' meetings (1 Cor. 14). He didn't throw out the baby with the dirty bath water. He taught them. It was all for the purpose of edification. The Lord wants us to excel in the edification of His body.

By revelation, the Lord showed us that carnal pastors are minimizing the grace of God because they're more concerned about self-image and how it looks and how it's perceived. We can't put young people in charge who are more concerned about image than the demonstration of the Spirit and the power of God. That is the danger and the warning from the Lord.

Ananias and Sapphira were stopped in their tracks because of the love of appearance (Acts 5). They wanted to appear as generous givers who had given away all their possessions. Self-worth and self-esteem keeps out the life of God and minimizes His grace.

It is time to return to our foundations so that we will not build in vain. It is time for those who are strong in the Word and who know the Spirit of God to pass these things on to the younger generation.

A Facebook friend of mine wrote me the following, concerning the Word and the Spirit that men of old carried:

"The men and women of old knew nothing of the extensiveness of error in the cotton-candy gospel of today. They nipped it in the bud. They stated without apology that without holiness we won't see the Lord. They knew scripture far better than today's Bible professors. Sister Pauline Parham, the daughter-in-law of Charles Parham, told me in Dallas in the early '80s that the old preachers knew the Word far better than the new generation, and powerful moves of the Spirit not seen today were common." — (Pauline Parham was Charles Parham's daughter in law. Charles Parham [1883-1929] was the first preacher to articulate Pentecostalism's distinctive doctrine of evidential tongues and to expand the movement.)

Add to that the following prophecy given to F.F. Bosworth's granddaughter:

"The ministers of your grandfather's day lit a Pentecostal fire that swept the world in their generation, but that fire has now died down to where only ashes and embers are left. But I am going to use your grandfather's recordings to breathe on these embers with the wind of My Spirit, and that fire will rekindle and sweep the world again in a new Pentecostal revival."

We are facing a huge famine today of the true word of the Lord, sound doctrine, and the genuine move of the Holy Spirit.

Our gospel lacks substance. Our salvation message is man-centered and defective. The theme of repentance is clearly absent. Excessive teachings on self-improvement and self-esteem have malnourished us. Our silence on sin and the Law of God in combination with the extreme hyper-grace and hyper-prosperity message has crippled the Church.

Many are waking up and realizing there is something terribly wrong.

Not only are we weak in sound doctrine, but the Spirit's demonstrations and power are so uncommon. Preachers are talking themselves and their audiences to death. Have we forgotten that *"the kingdom of God is not in talk but in power"*? (1 Cor. 4:20)

Yes, we will always need preaching and teaching, but the apostle Paul said that his *"preaching was not with enticing words of man's wisdom, but in demonstration of the Spirit and power of God."* This doesn't only mean that the demonstration of the Spirit and power of God will confirm the preaching of the Word itself but that the preaching is also to be a demonstration and that our words are to be filled with fire and utterances from heaven.

Where is the fire of God in our preaching?

Before Oral Roberts' departure to heaven, he was stirred by a vision from the Lord and emphatically stated, *"We've got to get back to preaching the cross with fire in our bellies!"* Men of old and past giants of the faith knew something about this.

And where is the preaching of the cross?

The constant popular emphasis on making the gospel relevant to our culture is obnoxious and misguided because it is rooted in the error that modern people must be reached on a humanistic level of their self-interest — that they are otherwise incapable of patiently hearing the gospel before becoming offended by its demands for righteousness and holiness. We must defeat that kind of thinking by showing that the real gospel is "the power of God unto salvation" for all people, for all time.

An extreme deluge of falsehood in both the Word and the Spirit are diluting the Church's influence and long-term fruit. Additionally, the cheap imitation of the gifts of the Holy Spirit and the gross superficial display of personal prophecy and prophetic ministry are keeping the Church hollow and empty. Forms and formulas, hype and heresy have robbed us of the true faith of our forefathers.

As we've already stated, concerning prophecy and prophetic ministry, what we've mostly witnessed has been visualizations and imaginings and just speaking whatever pops up in our heads, and calling it prophecy. In other, more serious cases, ministers have given over to familiar spirits through performance.

Anything that brings attention to flesh and the greatness of man is not an utterance from the Spirit of God. How many times have you turned on Christian television and heard some version of the following from another one of the many false or misguided prophets?

"You are about to be blessed and favored. The Lord has shown me that you are about to be wealthy beyond your dreams. You do not realize how much Daddy loves you and wants to bless you."

So many other such prophecies being touted from our nation's pulpits and over the airwaves are sickeningly similar. Still others are utterly meaningless, high-probability predictions.

There is a cry for the genuine gospel and the real power and demonstration of the Spirit. Many younger ministers and those of my generation are waking up to it and realizing that what they are doing is not working. Something is missing.

"Everywhere I go — and I mean everywhere — in Europe and Africa, younger ministers are approaching me and saying, 'This stuff we're preaching just does not work. Tell us something that works. Tell us about how to get ahold of the old-time power your father and mother walked in.'" — Dr. Ladonna Osborn, T.L. Osborn's daughter

The principles and power that men of old walked in are fading from this generation. As we've already stated, one of the problems we have is the lack of wisdom to blend the old and the new.

Let us read this Scripture carefully in two different translations:

"Therefore every scribe who has become a disciple of the kingdom of heaven is like the head of a household, who brings out of his treasure things that are new and fresh and things that are old and familiar" (Mt. 13:52 — Amp.).

Then He added, "Those experts in Jewish law who are now my disciples have double treasures — from the Old Testament as well as from the New!" (Mt. 13:52 – TLB)

One of the things Jesus is saying here is that knowledge of the Old Testament provides insight into Jesus' new message of the kingdom of God. In the same way, knowledge of what the past giants of the faith taught and practiced needs to be blended in with what God is doing and saying today. The wise scribe or householder will build on each truth that is revealed.

Excesses, extremes, and abuses will surely be manifest, but we must learn to garner the wheat into our spiritual storehouses and burn up the chaff. As one wise old man used to say, *"Have the sense of an old cow — eat the hay and leave the sticks."* We cannot afford to throw out the baby with the dirty bath water.

This is another area where many believers miss it. There are great truths on tongues and the operations of the Holy Spirit, on finances, on our authority as believers, and on faith and healing that have come to us in this generation, but because of some excesses and extremes, people throw everything out. Don't do that.

Recognizing the difference between the wheat and the chaff is the key. Being exposed to the wheat is vital in making the distinction. Just as bank tellers learn to distinguish counterfeit bills from the real by being familiar with the real, so it is with the things of the Spirit.

Blend the old with the new and have a balance of the true Word and the Spirit.

AN EARNEST APPEAL FOR A FULLER EXPRESSION OF CHRIST'S MINISTRY GIFTS

"And He Himself gave some to be apostles, some prophets, some evangelists, and some pastors and teachers, for the equipping of the saints for the work of ministry, for the edifying of the body of Christ, till we all come to the unity of the faith and of the knowledge of the Son of God, to a perfect man, to the measure of the stature of the fullness of Christ; that we should no longer be children, tossed to and fro and carried about with every wind of doctrine, by the trickery of men, in the cunning craftiness of deceitful plotting ... " (Eph. 4:11-14).

For the body of Christ to mature properly and fully, and to receive maximum edification, they need to be exposed to the five ministries God has set in the body of Christ — the apostle, the prophet, the evangelist, the pastor, and the teacher. The body of Christ also needs exposure to different types of meetings — teaching and training meetings, evangelistic meetings, prayer meetings, believers meetings (where all participate according to the leading of the Spirit — 1 Cor. 14:26), healing meetings, etc.

The Sunday-morning worship and teaching experience is simply not enough.

Many years ago, it was common for a ministry to conduct week-long meetings in a church. Even longer ago, early pioneers would go to a church and minister for several weeks at a time. Due to the busy-ness and pressures of our modern day culture, this is not so common any more. This is another example of the operation and methodology changing in every generation.

Today people can access ministries and meetings online and be fed and stirred in their faith that way. But do most Christians really do this? And for those who do, doesn't it still fall short of the scriptural admonition of not forsaking the assembling of ourselves together (Heb. 10:25)? And are we not missing something from the great decrease in face-to-face meetings that were more common in days of old?

"For I long to see you, that I may impart to you some spiritual gift, so that you may be established — that is, that I may be encouraged together with you by the mutual faith both of you and me" (Rom. 1:11-12).

"For what thanks can we render to God for you, for all the joy with which we rejoice for your sake before our God, night and day praying exceedingly that we may see your face and perfect what is lacking in your faith?" (1 Thes. 3:10-11)

Paul desired to minister face to face to these precious saints, so he could impart some spiritual gift to them, establish them, and perfect what was lacking in their faith. Today itinerant ministers are always looking for ways to make adjustments in our fast-changing culture in ministering to people without compromising their integrity, or the Word and ministry of the Holy Spirit. Part of the answer is in utilizing the media and the Internet in ministering to people online through blog posts, social networks, YouTube videos, podcasts, and webcasts, etc. We do some of that ourselves, but there is no substitute for face-to-face meetings.

I will say it again: For a full equipping and a maximum edification to take place in the saints, there has to be a full exposure to the five ministries that the Lord has set in the Church (Eph. 4:11) and in the manifestations of the Spirit that accompany such (1 Cor. 12:7-11). A majority of the Church has gradually departed from this standard. The pastor-teacher is prominent in local church ministry but the apostle, prophet, and evangelist not nearly as much anymore. And the mighty manifestations of the Holy Spirit are in decline in many of our modern churches.

Do we really understand that certain impartations of the Spirit of God can linger and effectually work in a person for months and cause a permanent transformation in them? Do we esteem the gathering of the saints to this measure and degree?

Of course, we esteem the pastoral ministry, and without it, we are all out of order. But, on the other hand, sometimes they are the most likely candidates to block or hinder what the Lord may want to do in a particular church or city or region, due to a personal agenda that may not be of the Lord at all. In interfacing with local churches and pastors for many years, I've witnessed the restrictions created by the systems of men and church cultures that exist today, which are not conducive to a move of God. It has been so for many years. That statement alone is the reason many ministers will choose to host neutral meetings in a city, rather than be confined to the restrictions put on by one local church.

On the other hand, pastors have a reason to be cautious when working with outside ministries because they've been taken advantage of by some. For example, one evangelist came into a medium-size local church I minister at regularly, hyped up the people, and took up his own offering and walked away with tens of thousands of dollars. This pastor friend of mine told me he will never have that minister back again.

Other men have an eccentric ministry, with doctrinal tangents and questionable ethics that make pastors very uncomfortable in cooperating with and promoting such ministries that come into their area.

The bottom line is for each church and ministry to follow God's plan for them individually and to operate in the highest form of ministry ethics, honor, and integrity.

HOLY GHOST FORUMS

One of the formats that meets the need for face-to-face ministry from the fivefold ministry gifts in a short span of time, while combining both diversity and liberty, are Holy Ghost Forums. These forums are schools of the Spirit where instruction, teaching, and demonstration are given according to 1 Cor. 14:26 through a team of seasoned ministers.

Imagine a forum like this in your city where the body of Christ is invited and local pastors and ministers are our special guests. Imagine a place where the Holy Spirit has free reign and there is training by precept and example of how to move with the Holy Spirit in demonstration and power.

What other setting is there where, in a two or three-day period, the body of Christ in a local area could be ministered to at a higher level by a small team of ministers all at once? This is true team ministry done decently and in order where one has a psalm, another has a teaching, and another has a tongue, a revelation, and an interpretation. I've always had a conviction that team ministry would be a restored dynamic of these last days just before Jesus returns.

In the New Testament, we see team ministry. After all, Jesus ministered with His disciples and sent them out two by two to minister as well. Paul ministered with Barnabas and then with Silas. Barnabas ministered with Judas. Paul seemed to always travel with not only one other minister but often with a team of others. After Philip preached a mighty revival in Samaria, Peter and John came down to help the multitudes receive the Holy Spirit.

Mark my words. This team-ministry dynamic of fivefold ministers will cause the level of power and anointing to increase, and it will diffuse the attention from being on one man or ministry all the time. We have not yet seen the measure of effectiveness and anointing that team ministry can produce if done correctly with wisdom and by the Spirit.

During a recent time of prayer, the Spirit of God spoke to my wife and me about the unwrapping of Christ's ministry gifts for greater glory. Then we read this in Billye Brim's book on prayer: *"You have never yet seen the operation of Christ's ministry gifts (Eph. 4:11), or what you call the gifts of the Spirit (1 Cor. 12:1-11), as they were designed to operate. But before Jesus comes, you shall see the fullness of the operation of these gifts as they were designed to function. They will adorn the Church to walk in glory."* I see this happening not only individually but in team dynamics as well.

May the great Holy Ghost have His way in the full expression of His gifts and ministries in this hour.

CHAPTER 21

HEALINGS AND MIRACLES:
THE KINGDOM OF GOD IS IN POWER

"For the kingdom of God is not in word, but in power" (1 Cor. 4:20).

I am a big proponent of the supernatural power of God. I came into it when I was baptized in the Holy Spirit shortly after my conversion. I will never understand men who reason away or dumb down the supernatural workings of God and His sacred gifts. I realize there are sensationalists and religious fanatics who abuse and misuse God's gifts and power, but that doesn't do away with the real. Once you've tasted the genuine move and power of the Holy Spirit, it is difficult to settle for anything else.

Jimmy Horton was a frontline soldier in the Vietnam War. While engaged in combat, he often thought of how he longed to hear a tongue and interpretation. You see, Jimmy was from a Spirit-filled church back home in America, where they had constant manifestations of these things. The other gifts of the Holy Spirit were in operation there as well.

When is the last time you witnessed a tongue and interpretation in a meeting? When is the last time you witnessed a genuine healing or deliverance in a meeting or in the marketplace? These manifestations should be common occurrences.

Years ago I was ministering in Gambia, West Africa. As I briefly mentioned earlier in this book, in one of the meetings, as the saints broke out in dancing and joy, a demon-possessed young man was struck by the power of God on the streets next to the facility. He froze and couldn't move. Finally, the men brought him into the meeting, and we cast the evil spirit out of him and then ministered salvation and the baptism of the Holy Spirit to him.

As I interviewed this young man afterwards, I became fascinated with his testimony. For 12 years, he'd been under the spell of Satan. From a very young age, demons unveiled the spirit world to him, as degree by degree, they possessed him.

I asked him many questions. I will not elaborate on the entire interview I had with him, but I want to enforce one main point that was very compelling to me. I asked him if he'd ever sought to be delivered from these demons. He told me that he'd visited many churches but that none could help him. As a matter of fact, instead of being helped, the demons in this young man often hurt the amateur exorcists.

For example, in the largest Charismatic church in the country, the demon in this man slapped the pastor and ransacked his office, repeatedly telling him that his church had no power to set him free. "All this church does is talk about money, and they don't live holy." the demon said. Can you believe a demon said that? Demons know churches. Demons know men. *"Jesus I know, Paul I know, but who are you?"* (Acts 19:15)

This incident made me wonder: How many of our churches are really a threat to Satan's kingdom? The evil spirit knew the real character of this church. They were not holy, and all they talked about was money. In other words, they were sinful and full of greed or covetousness.

This particular church believed in the supernatural, for they attempted to cast the evil spirit out of this young man, but they couldn't do it. You can't serve the devil and cast him out. A house divided against itself cannot stand (Mt. 12:25). Many churches, however, do not even believe in the supernatural. Others, like this one, profess to believe in it, but they don't live right, so they have no power with God. And there are still others who are just talking to themselves and making excuses for their lack of power.

Ministers will often tell you that these things happen as the Spirit wills. However, if your church hasn't had these manifestations in 10 or 20 years, it's not because the Spirit hasn't been willing. The problem is on the receiving end.

Some say, "You can't just turn these things on and off!" But I have found from experience that the Holy Spirit is always on. The question should be: Are you on or off?

When I was a student in Bible school, I learned about faith and the supernatural power of God. I had been saved only about two years, fresh out of the Roman Catholic Church, so I didn't know much about God's power. I heard of the exploits of men of old, but I was not satisfied with only reading of what they did. I learned that God is no respecter of persons, and He desires to use us all to minister His power to others. Immediately I began to put my faith into action. As I saw the ensuing results and witnessed people being healed and delivered, I was further ignited to do the works of Jesus (Jn. 14:12).

The difference for me in procuring results came when I received a working understanding of faith and learned the various methods of how Jesus ministered to people. I learned the difference between ministering by faith and ministering with the anointing. I learned that Jesus ministered healing and deliverance primarily in three different ways: 1) through faith; 2) through the anointing of the gifts of the Holy Spirit, and 3) through a transfer of power that God anointed Him with.

Unless believers receive a clear understanding of how God works, they will often be hindered from stepping forth boldly in ministering the power of God to others. I spent countless hours studying the ministry and works of Jesus. For example, I remember listening to a 12-tape audio series and taking notes on each lesson.

My greatest influence was the life and ministry of the late Kenneth E. Hagin. Although he was a tremendous teacher, he was not a theologian or a lecturer. Most theologians and Bible-college lecturers today have never walked in the supernatural power of God, and honestly, most don't even believe in it. Brother Hagin, however, was a man of great faith who walked in the supernatural power of God for most of his life. What a great solid foundation I received from him! This one association early in my Christian life made the biggest impact on me and my ministry. For many years now, I have continued to see results of God's healing and delivering power.

The healings and miracles I've seen are too numerous to tell, but over the years I've highlighted and made note of some of the more outstanding ones.

When I was a young missionary in Liberia, I visited a young, 15-year-old boy who had been hospitalized with tetanus and was being cared for in the intensive care unit. I believe he got it from stepping on a rusty nail. In some cases, this disease can be fatal.

During my first visit to see him, all I did was pump him with faith in God. I gave him two or three scriptures to meditate on and confess. I was very authoritative and strong with him, looking him right in the eyes. I knew that, if he doubted, it wouldn't work for him, so I blasted the doubt out of him. His mother was there with him, and I basically gave her the same instructions. I learned that from watching other seasoned ministers do it, but I thoroughly believed it myself. I left this boy confessing the Word of God and told him I'd be back to check on him the next day.

When I returned the next day, I didn't even have to ask how he was doing. Both he and his mother began to cry when they saw me, while simultaneously confessing the scriptures I had taught them. Overnight they had seen marked improvement. Their faith had taken hold. I encouraged them to continue to hold fast to the Word of God and again promised them I'd return to check on them the next day.

When I returned for the third day, the nurse told me that he had been discharged and was completely well. Praise the Name of Jesus! Once again I had put to work the faith I had learned from my fathers and teachers. My greatest joy was to see this young boy and his mother rejoicing in God's goodness shown to them.

In addition to the aforementioned deliverance of the demon-possessed boy and the boy with tetanus, here are a couple of other outstanding testimonies shared in their own words:

1.   For 13 months I suffered from chronic pain and limited mobility due to a severe neck-and-back injury from falling at a cheerleading camp. I had muscular/skeletal damage. The vertebrae in my neck were compressed, nerves were pinched and muscles were in a chronic spasm. I was on 28 pain pills and meds every day just so that I could function to some degree. I was receiving physical therapy, aquatic therapy, massage therapy, and chiropractic care.

Brother Bert Farias and his wife, whom we affectionately called "Sister C," ministered to me and prayed for healing. I could feel heat on the top of my head, and as they prayed the heat moved down through my neck, down my back, into my legs and out of my feet, and I was instantly healed. The pain was gone. All gone. There hadn't been one second in 13 months that I had been without hard pain, and now the pain was out of my body. They told me to try to move and do something I wasn't able to do. I turned my head left and right, up and down. Healed!! I leaned over and touched the ground. Healed!! No pain, and I had full range of motion and mobility. I ran, I skipped, I jumped, and I did cartwheels — All things I wasn't able to do before. Praise Jesus — I was healed!!!

I returned to the doctor shortly after for them to check on my X-rays, and, sure enough, all was well — my vertebrae were realigned and no longer compressed. God is good!!! So thankful for these dear ones who prayed for me and still amazed 15 years later at how God healed me — (Summer Daniel)

2.   My husband and I had tried to conceive for three years. We finally sought out help from a doctor who informed us that it was impossible for us to have kids (based on his extensive testing). Brother Bert laid hands on us and prayed for us while we were on a 30-day missions trip to Africa. He spoke words from the Lord straight to our hearts regarding children. The words that he spoke were just the opposite of the grim news the doctor had given us. The Lord used

Brother Bert to deliver His Word to us. He never knew what the doctor had said but was used mightily as a messenger of the Lord to prove that nothing is impossible with God. It was a powerful time of ministry. Our son was born nine months later! Our twin daughters were born four years after that — (Nancy Hale)

Here's a more recent one that happened just a few weeks ago, told by the aunt of the individual involved:

3.   On September 1st, my niece, who is very dear to my heart, was rushed to the emergency room with a breathing issue. Upon arrival, things looked very grim. She had a neck brace and a breathing tube down her throat. Many tests were done but to no avail. Then the fevers started, and her temperature shot up to 104 degrees. The machine was doing almost all her breathing. Her heart rate and pulse, as well as her blood pressure, were extremely high.

She was taken to the cardiac care unit, where she lay unconscious until September 5th, when a prayer cloth was taken from Brother Bert's body and placed on her body. Within a half an hour, things started to change. Her body began thrashing, and she came to herself, but because of the thrashing, they had to sedate her again. But on the morning of September 7th, they permanently removed her breathing tube, and she is a living miracle. Her first words were: "Am I going to live?"

Praise be to God!

Time will fail me to tell you of all the other incredible healings, deliverances, and miracles I've witnessed in my own life and ministry through the years — from fractured and crippled limbs, to blindness and deafness, to deliverance from spirits of infirmity, and even some unusual manifestations. But it's not over. I'm looking for more. These are the last days, and God has promised us that the glory of the latter house would be greater, the miracles and power of God would be greater, and the anointing of the Holy Spirit would be stronger as we near the Lord's return. Let's get after it! Let's exercise our faith and believe God to do great exploits for His glory.

How much value do you place on these things? In a day when church leaders are moving into a seeker-friendly type of philosophy, the true power of Pentecost and the gifts of the Holy Spirit are no longer held in high esteem. I asked an old-time Pentecostal minister what he thought of seeker-friendly churches, and he frankly told me that he thought it was a disgrace to God. It's telling God that we don't need His power and precious gifts to get the job done. It's telling God that we can do it by ourselves and we don't need His help.

How can we have more of these gifts operating in our lives and in our churches?

First of all, the Word instructs us not to be ignorant of the supernatural gifts of God (1 Cor. 12:1). Learn from the learned, not the unlearned. Seek out those who teach and demonstrate these gifts, not those who deny them. It is so important to be in a faith-filled environment and to be exposed to a solid and balanced example of the demonstration of the Spirit and power of God.

Secondly, the Word admonishes us to covet these gifts and the power of God (1 Cor. 12:31; 14:1). To "covet" is to have a strong desire, equivalent to lust in the physical realm. Desire these gifts, and expect the manifestation of them.

Thirdly, let us pray for these gifts as the early Church did and learn to yield to them when they manifest (Acts 4:29-31). But again, it is important to learn from others who have gone before you and are ministering consistently in these areas. We must have the example of it because these things are better caught than taught.

I've said it throughout this book, and it is the very theme of this book, that if the move of the Spirit is not passed on to this next generation, it will be lost. Let's wake up to this light and walk therein. Get turned on — because the Holy Ghost is always on.

CHAPTER 22

HOW TO BE ON FIRE FOR GOD

This chapter is not what you think. I'm not going to tell you to read the Word more, pray and worship more, share Jesus more, or repent. Those things are great and should be a regular part of our Christian lives, but I am going to unlock a mystery to the fire of God that perhaps you've never thought of or known before.

My son coined a phrase when he was in public high school: "When Jesus becomes real, everything changes." That phrase registered really strongly in my spirit when my son spoke it, and we included it in a father-son book we wrote together (_My Son, My Son_).

Think about the individuals Jesus touched, healed, delivered, and revealed Himself to. Most of them exploded with fire at the personal revelation of not only what Jesus did for them but, ultimately, who He was.

For example, the woman at the well, to whom we've already referred in this book, exploded with the revelation of Jesus as Messiah and testified with fire to the men of her city.

"The woman then left her water pot, went her way into the city, and said to the men, 'Come, see a Man who told me all things that I ever did. Could this be the Christ?'" (John 4:28-29)

The leper, after being cleansed and made whole, and told to keep quiet about it, instead exploded with fire and blazed abroad what Jesus had done for him.

"But he went out, and began to publish it much, and to blaze abroad the matter, insomuch that Jesus could no more openly enter into the city, but was without in desert places: and they came to him from every quarter" (Mark 1:45, KJV).

After the crucifixion, death, and resurrection of the Lord Jesus Christ, the two disciples on the road to Emmaus were set on fire when Jesus revealed Himself to them at the breaking of bread. It was in that place of intimate fellowship and communion with the Lord that their eyes were opened to see Him. Blessed are those believers who maintain an intimacy with the Lord.

"As He sat at supper with them, He took the bread, blessed it and broke it, and gave it to them. Then their eyes were opened, and they recognized Him. And He vanished out of their sight. They said to each other, "Did not our hearts burn within us while He talked to us on the way and while He opened the Scriptures to us?' They rose up and returned to Jerusalem at once. And they found the eleven and those who were with them assembled together, saying, 'The Lord has risen indeed, and has appeared to Simon!' Then they reported what had happened on the way, and how He was recognized by them in the breaking of the bread" (Luke 24:30-35).

The hearts of these two disciples burned at the revelation of who Jesus was. But notice what they did.

It was late in the evening, and they had just walked about seven miles from Jerusalem that day. They were tired. But when Jesus was revealed to them in the breaking of bread, they were energized and set on fire. So what did they do? They went all the way back to Jerusalem to testify of the risen, living Jesus. And I bet you they didn't walk but ran!

The basis for getting on fire for God is a heart-rending revelation of the Lamb of God. You might say, "I've already had a revelation of Jesus, and I'm saved. But I've lost my fire."

The bottom line for staying on fire for God is to be continually filled and baptized into the implications of who Jesus is to you personally.

THE REVELATION OF THE LOVE OF CHRIST

The love of God was demonstrated throughout Jesus' ministry, but the height of that love was demonstrated on the cross. The cup Jesus prayed over in the garden of Gethsemane (Mt. 26, Mk. 14, Lk. 22), and eventually drank, is the climax of the cross of Jesus Christ. Although it happened before the cross, Jesus won the victory in the garden when He chose to drink that cup.

We tend to forget about that cup. It was filled with the wrath of God's fury against all sin. God rolled the sin of the ages and the sin of all mankind upon Jesus. Visiting that reality of the spotless and innocent Lamb of God should pierce your soul and reignite your fire.

The Western church has had a veil over the eyes of their heart because they've wandered from the purity of the gospel of the cross. The cup is a part of the cross, and it acts like a sword that cuts away the scales that cover our spiritual eyes, so that we can see more of Christ.

When we see the fearfulness of God's wrath and the exceeding sinfulness of our sin in that cup and how Jesus drank it, we will be awakened and compelled to live solely and wholly for His glory and the reward of His sacrifice.

Scripture tells us that, in the garden of Gethsemane, Jesus sweat great drops of blood (Lk. 22:44). It was not just a trickle of blood; the Greek bears forth the meaning of "large, thick drops of clotted blood" falling to the ground. Again, this happened before He ever went to the cross.

In the garden, Jesus was not agonizing over the physical suffering of the crucifixion that He was soon to face, but the fierceness of God's wrath that was about to be poured upon Him for our sin. He knew the Old Testament Scriptures concerning the lambs being offered up as burnt offerings for the sins of the people. He knew about the fire of God's wrath that consumed those burnt offerings.

He knew of the Father's plan that He had agreed to in eternity past to become the Lamb offering for man's sin. He knew the Scriptures concerning the *"cup of horror and desolation"* (Ezek. 23:33) that was filled with the wine of God's wrath (Jer. 25:15). He knew Isaiah's prophecy in chapter 53 of how He would be *"stricken, smitten of God, and afflicted"* with the punishment for our sins (Is. 53:4).

He was wrestling in the garden with these images flowing and reeling in his mind.

He purposed to do the will of the Father and drink that cup. Why did He do it? Because He saw you and me. He didn't want us to have to drink it.

He didn't want us to drink of the wine of the wrath of God, which is poured out in full strength into the cup of the Father's indignation. He didn't want us to be tormented with fire and brimstone in His presence and in the presence of God's holy angels forever (Rev. 14:10). He didn't want us to *"totter and be mad"* from drinking the cup of God's wrath (Jer. 25:16).

This He did—all for you and all for me. This glorious revelation of His amazing love is what God has chosen to transform you and set you on fire.

Now, take a deep, long look at the cup, and be ignited with an unquenchable fire and passion for the Lamb and for the reward of His sacrifice.

"We love Him because He first loved us" (1 Jn. 4:19).

Can we give Him any less?

CHAPTER 23

MY STORY OF MOVING WITH THE GLORY

My last college roommate, Donny, and I got saved around the same time. After being saved, he began fellowshipping at a Baptist church and invited me to join him for a service. I went and enjoyed the solid salvation message that is common to Baptist doctrine.

Around the same time, the man who had led me to the Lord invited me to attend a Pentecostal Bible study. Well, guess what? I brought my roommate Donny with me. Like me, he enjoyed the Word but was uncomfortable with the Pentecostal display of exuberance — and that funny language they called "tongues." I was not uncomfortable at all but rather intrigued by it. I saw it laid out in the Scriptures, but already having been somewhat influenced by traditional Baptist doctrine, Donny couldn't see it.

The more he associated with non-Pentecostal people who criticized tongues, the farther away he got from being open and teachable to accepting and receiving the baptism in the Holy Ghost with the initial physical evidence of speaking in tongues. The big lesson here is that our associations can hinder or help us in receiving all God has for us in our Christian lives. I was a witness of this early on in my walk with the Lord.

Shortly thereafter, I was baptized in the Holy Ghost and began speaking in other tongues regularly. I have enjoyed that free-flowing stream of blessing, revelation, and power in my life since those early days. My friend Donny went in the opposite direction, and to my knowledge, has never been filled with the Holy Ghost.

About 18 months later, I chose to obey God's calling on my life to attend Rhema Bible Training Center (now College). The Christian folks in the area I lived warned me of associating myself with those "name it and claim it" prosperity preachers. On the inside, I knew those folks were mistaken and seeing things through only the small lens of the environment they were in. They were seeing the dirty bath water, but I saw the baby. I also knew that most of them would never grow spiritually beyond a certain point because of their associations.

While I was at Bible school I received an impartation from the late Kenneth E. Hagin — an impartation of a spirit of faith, boldness, and the supernatural. I learned great foundational truths on the gifts and ministries of the Holy Spirit, healing, love, prayer, the authority of the believer, and many redemptive realities. I caught a wave of the supernatural that launched me into fruitful ministry.

In Bible school, one of our first special speakers we had was the late Dr. Lester Sumrall. He was 70 years old at that time, and he told the students how the Lord had allowed him to be in every major move of God throughout his life. He went on to explain how every move of God is like a wave out at sea. Every wave has an end, and most Christians will ride one wave onto the seashore until they dry up. Dr. Sumrall compared many Christians' lives to denominations that were birthed in revival but then dried up. He told us that, as soon as a wave heads onto the seashore, you should be looking for the next one to jump on.

Dr. Sumrall even explained to us how he'd lost close friendships over these issues because some chose to stay on the same wave, or denomination, which eventually dried up, while he kept moving on with God. Once again, associations are one of the greatest influences that determine a person's spiritual level in God.

I totally grasped this wisdom and received it right there and then; I prayed that the Lord would keep me in the center of all he was doing on the earth. After I graduated from Bible school, God sent me overseas as a missionary. Who would've known that, once again, Dr. Sumrall would be one of our first special speakers on the mission field in the nation of Liberia at our annual Bible school convention and graduation ceremony?

While there, he told us that this was one of the greatest moves of God he'd ever witnessed in all his years of ministry. I was surprised and wondered why he said that concerning our team and the ministry we planted there under the leadership of the late Russ Tatro. He said it was because he'd never seen so many denominations under one roof. He called that a great move of God. Our Bible schools had students from nearly every denomination in the country. We were in the middle of that move and didn't even realize how great it was.

Then my wife and I moved to the small Muslim nation of Gambia to pioneer another work. A resident pastor in this country told me if we started a Bible school there, we might have 10 students. That discouraged me at first, but we had learned to pray and to walk in faith and obedience. We started with 200 students, and the ministry prospered. The door to the gospel was closing in that nation, but God kicked it open through our labors in the Lord and those of others. We and our national team rode that wave for several years in that country before the Lord sent us back to America.

In America, I received a call to be a part of another great wave of revival that was mounting up in Pensacola, Florida, which became known as the Brownsville Revival. Some were not too sure about this wave, either, as it received heavy criticism from denominations. Even some of my Rhema friends from Bible school days were concerned about it because it was a different wave from what they were used to. But we knew it was God, and we rode it and enjoyed it while it lasted. In a five-year span, four million visitors came from around the world, and 150,000 first-time salvations were recorded in that great revival and move of God. We were privileged to train and equip many who came from all over America and around the world to the school of ministry that was spawned from the revival there.

Many who were a part of that move are longing for the past and praying for another wave like that one, but no two waves are exactly the same. Don't try to imitate what the Lord did in the past, but be engaged in what He is doing now.

God is always moving. Smith Wigglesworth said, *"I have revival everywhere I go because I live full."* This is what Christians must understand. As I've been saying, God's plan under the new covenant is for every believer to live a Spirit-filled life. You cannot do that without being baptized in the Holy Ghost and speaking in new tongues.

Go back to the beginning of this chapter. What would've happened if I'd decided to side with my friend Donny and his church association and resist the baptism of the Holy Ghost? I would've never been privileged to ride the waves I've ridden all these many years of ministry. Two different choices resulted in two very different destinies. I rejoice that my friend Donny is saved and probably still loves the Lord today, but how different would it have been for him had he embraced and received the baptism in the Holy Ghost?

Every man has as much of God as He wants. Your associations will either put something in you or take it out of you. They will make you better or worse. They will lift you up higher in God or try to keep you at or below their level. Most people will attempt to create your world for you, and they will always create it too small.

Move with God, believer! Who cares what your best friend says? You are not accountable to him but to God. Who cares what your favorite preacher says? I know many good preachers and theologians who know little to nothing about the Holy Ghost and moving with God in the supernatural.

What will my church think? Who cares what your dead church thinks? If it's dead, it stinks. Your church may even have started in revival but perhaps is now only an empty shell of what it once was — a monument memorializing the past. Jesus said, *"Let the dead bury the dead."* You go on and move with God.

Move with God, preacher! Who cares what your dead church members say? Who cares what your peers think? It's better to obey God than man. Who cares about the church's traditions that contradict the Word of God? Who cares what your denominational authorities say? If you know it's God, flow with it! He will bless you for your obedience and take care of you.

If you don't know how to move with God, it is time to associate with those who do.

THE SUPERNATURAL: GOD IS WAITING ON YOU

"I used to go down there to that church when they had the power," said one businessman. Some elders in the church thought they'd be able to draw the businessmen in by toning down on the speaking in tongues and the power of God. But this one businessman responded: "I'll just go back to my dead church because this one is just as dead."

That would be funny if it wasn't so pathetic. Churches are pulling back on the very element of the supernatural that is universally craved by man. From as far back as the book of Genesis, the supernatural was active and operative and translated Enoch, called out Abraham, lifted up Joseph, and delivered Israel from the bondage of Egypt through a series of signs and wonders, under the supernatural leadership of Moses.

God's purpose in leading Israel out of bondage was to separate them from the dead gods of Egypt and compel them to worship the living God of Abraham, Isaac, and Jacob. When the supernatural ceased to operate, Israel returned to idolatry and heathenism. And they were brought back into fellowship with Jehovah only after a series of stunning supernatural manifestations. There is no parallel in human history to the operation of the miraculous power of God working through the lives and characters of the Old Testament.

As we move into the New Testament, we see the Lord Jesus Christ stepping into public ministry by way of the supernatural. The apostles he chose and disciples he trained — and even some outside his circle — ministered in the supernatural (Lk. 9:49). The early Church was commanded to wait in Jerusalem for the outpouring of the Holy Spirit until they were endued with power from on high (Lk. 24:49).

Every revival since the day of Pentecost that has honored the Lord has been a revival of the supernatural. Throughout Church history, when the Church came alive and into fellowship with God, they experienced the supernatural power of God in various ways. But today we have substituted Madison Avenue tactics and the methods of men to draw men to God. How pathetic! How is it, brethren, that we have come to this? Who has bewitched you? Having begun in the Spirit, do you now resort to fleshly based means derived from the wisdom of men to build the Church of Jesus Christ?

Now, ignorance of the power of God is one thing, but there are entire full-gospel denominations that have departed from the supernatural. I've preached in some of them, and they are as dry as last year's bird's nest. Either that, or they just make a lot of noise with little substance. Get ahold of yourselves, Reverends, and return to your Pentecostal heritage.

Some may say, "Well, we believe in the power of God, and we've been praying for it," but that is only half of the equation. You think you are waiting on God, but He is actually waiting on you.

You don't have to wait for the supernatural. Go out and put the supernatural to work. Step out and loose your faith!

"Oh, yes, many have asked and asked and asked with tears, with fastings, with loud cries. Why don't you come Lord? Why don't you move among us? And they ask and ask and ask again. "Come, oh Lord! Come, oh Lord! And yet thus saith the Lord, 'I've given you My Word. Why don't you act on My Word? I've given you My Spirit. He's within you. Why don't you listen to Him? Why don't you rise up in the power of the Spirit and go forth to do what I've called you to do?

"And if you'll obey Me, then surely I will manifest Myself through thee, and I will cause signs to be wrought by thy hands, and you'll see and man will see the hand of the Lord at work among his own. And great, great, great things shall be wrought, and many shall be turned toward the Lord. And many who sit in darkness shall come and walk in the light, and the glory of the Lord shall shine around upon thee and the manifestation of His power shall come upon thee and among thee. And even the eyes of many shall be opened, and they will say, 'Why, I saw Jesus standing by that man as he ministered.' And the eyes of others in the

congregation and even sinners will say, 'I saw an angel walk down the aisle.' Yea and great shall be the manifestation of His power and great shall be the rejoicing of His saints."(Holy Spirit-inspired utterance)

Step out in faith and cooperate with God. Step into the supernatural. Glory to God!

PART II
PREACH THE WORD

CHAPTER 24

RESTORING THE PROPHETIC DISTINCTION AND GLORIOUS PROCLAMATION OF THE CHURCH

"I charge you therefore before God and the Lord Jesus Christ, who will judge the living and the dead at His appearing and His kingdom: Preach the word! Be ready in season and out of season. Convince, rebuke, exhort, with all longsuffering and teaching. For the time will come when they will not endure sound doctrine, but according to their own desires, because they have itching ears, they will heap up for themselves teachers; and they will turn their ears away from the truth, and be turned aside to fables" (2 Tim. 4:1-4).

A lukewarm spirit incomparable to anything I've witnessed in my day has overtaken so many professing Christians. Many are falling away from a vibrant and living Christianity as the world gets all their attention. No longer are Christians, in general, open to penetrating and piercing preaching. They are afraid of truth that warns and convicts.

Years ago, when I first started preaching, I got discouraged after a meeting, because no one responded to what I thought was a real word from God. The elderly pastor who had been around in the tent meetings of old with such names as Oral Roberts and Jack Coe encouraged me. He told me that if my message had been preached back in that day, the people would've made a run for the altar before I had even finished preaching. Those words encouraged me and gave me a fresh perspective that it was not that my preaching was un-anointed but that the character of the age had changed.

Decades ago people wanted to hear about sin and true grace, the law, the cross, and the real gospel, repentance, holiness, and sanctification. Christians even enjoyed hell, fire, and brimstone messages. Today we've substituted "Happy Christianity." If it hurts the flesh and the feelings, people don't want it. They want flowery-sounding words that tell them how wonderful they are, and how God will prosper them and make all their dreams come true. Worse still, is that preachers accommodate their itching ears with more dainties for the sweet tooth. I fear that we are not properly preparing the majority of the Church for the day of battle when they may have to endure strong persecution, hardness, and tribulation.

The important thing now in the marketplace of Christianity is to be a success, to be somebody, to have material goods, and enjoy the good life, which, to many Christians, simply means fulfilling the American dream of happiness, peace, and prosperity. Instead of having gatherings where prayer, repentance, and revival are the focus, the popular notion is to emphasize entertainment, technology, arts, and culture. Of course, we attach a nice little pep talk to it, using some Scriptures. And if a minister already has a large building and a large following, people will believe whatever he says. There is such a spiritual poverty on the listeners, who swallow anything a popular, elevated teacher says without ever checking the Scriptures to see if it is really so.

The glory of preaching has diminished in these modern times. We've forgotten that the Church is the only entity on the earth that carries the responsibility and stewardship of public proclamation. A value and esteem for Holy Scripture has diminished. Paralyzed by worldly distractions, it is only a minority now who really savor the living Word.

The Church has lost its prophetic distinction in the world because of its own worldliness. Like Samson, we've fallen into the lap of Delilah and allowed her to take our strength. Ministers have failed to function effectively in their high priestly role of prayer and the Word. The lethargy in our pulpits has been passed down to our pews.

We have mastered the art of performing services at the expense of incarnational preaching, where men are moved upon by the Holy Spirit and speak inspired utterances from God. Men are more interested today in the preservation of their ministries than the edification of the Church and the salvation of men. Penetrating preaching that brings a consciousness of man's condition before God and eternal realities has clearly diminished from mainstream Christianity. This again is a sure sign that the Church has left her first love, and the honor of the Lord is no longer the treasure of many ministers and saints.

When our vision of the Lord increases, when we see Him in the beauty of holiness and in His awesome majesty, we will catch fire inwardly, and the exaltation of Spirit proclamation will be restored in our day. When it does, the hearer's conception of God will increase, and His purposes will be esteemed as worthy of our time, labor, and investment. A vibrant affection for the Lord, along with a fresh zeal and an eagerness to serve Him and do His will, shall grip the people of God again, and they will go forth truly empowered as faithful witnesses in these last days.

In the early Church, the apostles were fit to proclaim eternal realities because they had been with Jesus and continued to devote themselves to prayer and the Word (Acts 4:13, 6:4). They recognized that if fervent, unceasing, Spirit-wrought prayer should decrease in them and in the Church, the giving and receiving of the Word of God would also decrease.

Let us return to the old paths and true foundations of our faith. Let us preoccupy ourselves with the glory of God. Let us pray the glories of what Ephesians 1:16-23 and 3:14-21 promise us so that we may be filled with all the fullness of God.

CHAPTER 25

SEEKER-FRIENDLY CHURCH TEMPLATE MODEL FAILING OUR YOUTH

I received an unsettling report one time of two pastors who, in their attempts to reach more youth and college-age students, started toning down on all things Holy Spirit related and personal holiness, for fear that it would offend the young. How can you possibly call yourself a New Testament church pastor and come to this conclusion? From where does this persuasion come?

Unfortunately, this has become a disturbing trend across the country in many churches. Church worship resembles a rock-concert performance (honestly, even Charismatics and Pentecostals know so little about true worship). Singers and musicians are like celebrities. Some of them even lead immoral lifestyles, and nothing is ever said.

Robotic, predictable services are the norm. Being tolerant of anyone living in sin is actually promoted. This is now the pop culture of a multitude of churches.

One honest question: What happens when youth discover the real Jesus, the real gospel, and the raw power of God? Let me inform you now before it all comes down. There will be a mass exodus from these apostate churches.

Apostate??? Isn't that a bit strong — to label them "apostate"? Any church that has left New Testament Christianity, which hinges on godly character and conduct as well as the demonstration of the Spirit and power of God, is apostate. Any church that has left the wisdom of God and put their faith in the wisdom and philosophies of men is a traitor to the highest cause.

A second report came in right on the heels of this first one of a senior pastor and his staff from a large church returning from a

155

Christian conference supposedly armed with this new and higher wisdom to grow their church to mega-proportions.

Once again, as is becoming the pattern for so many churches now, they implemented drastic measures to remove anything and everything that resembles the manifestations of the Holy Spirit and the power of God. They stifled every prayer meeting in the church with guidelines and limitations void of any liberty of the Spirit. They changed the culture of the church into a coffee house atmosphere and made the uncommon so common — bringing sacred things to a base level. Such irreverence seems to be the norm.

Many older people with spiritual sense who had been in this particular church for years are now leaving. It is hard to believe. The only sensible explanation is that there has been a thick cloud of deception that church leaders are being sucked into that has made them delusional.

The seeker-friendly church template prides itself on doing church services so as not to offend anyone. It is consumer based and designed to draw and attract the multitudes who want to relate to Christianity without being delivered from their sins, and adhering to the demands of Jesus for being His true followers.

Frankly, all this ideology does is cause youth to see God only as a divine therapist. It results in many young people thinking that God simply wants them to feel good, do good, and be told how great and wonderful they are.

Even adults don't expect much from church youth pastors any more. They just simply hope that they can somehow keep their kids off drugs and away from pre-marital sex. And if they find out they're gay, well, just love and accept them anyway. There is very little regard for what the Lord thinks and what His Word actually says.

The real responsibility lies with parents and pastors for inspiring youth. But what are they doing to inspire them? They are unwittingly passing down a watered-down version of Christianity to them. Youth apathy is to be blamed on adults and church leadership.

Most churches don't give youth enough to be wholly passionate about. The Christianity a majority of them are being fed does not fuel them with fire.

Most young people are embracing a nebulous belief in God, and yet statistics show an increase in youth passion to make the world a better place. We think young people want ice cream and cake, but they actually want steak and potatoes.

Meanwhile, Muslims are training their youth for combat, and dying for their cause of world domination, while we are teaching our young people to be nice.

The radical faith of our leaders and elders is what will convey more to their children and youth than a multitude of sermons and nice talks. It has to register with our youth and children that faith is supposed to make you live radically different.

Let us rid ourselves of these humanistic philosophies and vain deceits. Teaching our young people to obey God rather than man is not going to offend them. Opposing man-made laws that contradict the Word of God and even encouraging civil disobedience toward our antichrist government and schools is not going to turn off our youth. Addressing the core of our nation's problems will not drive them away. On the contrary, this will actually open the door to their hearts. They already blame the government for destroying their future. It may look hip and cool to some preachers to remain silent, but many youth consider them traitors.

Pastors, it is high time to openly preach the entire message of Jesus Christ, including the cross, the Blood of Jesus, and hell. This will touch our youth deeply.

Youth want raw truth. They sense impending disaster, and their hope and optimism of a bright future is being sucked from them. They know they need something eternal that will never fade away. They need a cause far greater than themselves. They need something more than the American dream of health, wealth, and happiness. They want rock-solid ground to stand on, not fantasy-land sinking sand.

Getting out of God's way is our greatest challenge. Letting go of our own thimble-sized earthly wisdom and giving God control is not so easy for many pro-activist, high-strategist, type-A personalities. Youth want the power of God to demonstrate to them God's personal love and reality. This will make evangelists out of them. They will tell their friends about Jesus.

If you design your services and meeting times around the Holy Ghost and the power of God, our youth will not be spooked. What a crock of lies to even think that! Instead there will be a look of awe and wonder when real miracles start happening.

Forget about trying to "relate" to youth. This philosophy is overrated. Don't waste your planning on trying to create an atmosphere where youth feel you are being relevant. Youth feel a huge let-down when they go to church and are not challenged.

"The millennial generation's much-talked-about departure from church might lead those of us over 30 to conclude that they have little interest in Jesus. Nothing could be further from the truth.

"Unfortunately, their spiritual coming of age has coincided with many Protestant pastors relying on a consumer business model to grow and sustain their churches. This template for doing church and the millennials' hunger for authenticity has caused an ideological collision."— D.G.

May this collision reach unprecedented proportions until this generation realizes that the modern, milquetoast brand of Christianity has cheated them and ripped them off.

It is then that they will run to Jesus.

CHAPTER 26

BRING BACK THE OLD ANOINTINGS: HOW LONG WILL WE BE SATISFIED WITH HAPPY, SHALLOW REVIVALS?

Many of our so-called modern revivals are happy but shallow. This is of deep concern to me, for I am not seeing the old anointings anymore. My heart grieves especially for the young people who have never witnessed the real power of God.

Honestly, some things I see today are appalling. That old teaching that we are free from the Law has raised its ugly head again. Certainly, we are free from the Law written on stone, but we are not free from the Law that is written in our hearts.

In a time when repentance is needed the most, we have teachings sweeping the land that tell Christians they don't need to repent. In a day when there is a deplorable lack of holiness in the Church, we are being told that we are already holy enough through Christ's sacrifice (2 Cor. 7:1). In an hour when we sadly lack God's power, we are oversaturated with Church conferences that focus on numbers. Whatever it takes to grow numerically seems to be the cry of every powerless pastor.

Let me remind you that revival is not buildings full of people but people full of God.

Call me old school if you want to, but I see far too much irreverence, levity, frivolous behavior, a lack of holiness and sanctification, and a far-too-easy backsliding in the modern Church, which, frankly, is coming from hearing another gospel.

For the Pentecostal and Charismatic, our baptisms of the Holy Ghost are also too shallow. And we don't even speak in tongues any more, or we relegate it to the back room. Pentecostals seem to be growing in number, but where is the power?

Things have got to change, and it starts with ministers. If enough of us do not change, people will go underground and find another way. We will have more nones-and-dones, unchurched and de-churched among the multitudes.

Let's talk about our movement.

Is it still a movement, or have we been grounded? Are we really in revival or in a rut? Is it a mighty flowing river that brings refreshing, or has it become a swamp full of stench?

There was a time when Pentecostal meant something. In old-fashioned Pentecostal meetings, you weren't supposed to know what was going to happen next. When led by seasoned, mature men of spiritual stature, there was order, but there was also power and life. Today, it's five songs, a prayer, an offering, announcements, and a sermon, plus maybe another prayer at the end. Such routine and predictability!

Thus the reason many are leaving our local churches. They are bored to death — at least, the spiritual ones are. Oh, they're not leaving God; they're only leaving the church to find God. Ouch! I know it hurts to hear that.

As I stated earlier, at one time, Pentecostal meetings were nothing less than the gate of heaven. It was a meeting with God.

Repentance is our deepest need. Without repentance men's hearts are not touched, broken, melted, or moved. The result is hypocrisy and superficiality. There are many who still receive the Word with joy, but they lack depth or have no root. And so they are not fit for the day of tribulation or persecution (Mat. 13:5, 20-21). Through soft and non-repentance preaching, many pastors are lulling their people to sleep and actually grooming them to miss the rapture of the Church and be martyrs in the great day of tribulation (based on the pre-tribulation view).

You can easily tell where there has been true repentance. The one great characteristic is a love for the Word. *"Great peace have those who love Your Law, and nothing causes them to stumble"* (Ps. 119:165). If you're still easily offended, you have never repented as you should.

"Then He began to rebuke the cities in which most of His mighty works had been done, because they did not repent" (Mat. 11:20).

We desperately need miracles and the power of God, but as the Scripture above indicates, that alone does not guarantee repentance. Neither is it in what we say or don't say. We can say the sweetest things or the most terrible things with still no guarantee of repentance. Some will remain indifferent and never be affected. It is the Spirit that we need to produce repentance in men's hearts.

The call is to pray and to preach with the Spirit.

Jesus wept over the cities who had not repented because He knew of the judgment that was coming (Mt. 23). When is the last time you heard a message on judgment? Most preachers today have never been to the Judgment Seat. They will never preach it until they've trembled before it themselves. Today religion is happier to speak of universal salvation and a pie in the sky for each of us, regardless of the road traveled to get there.

Without the Holy Spirit, you will make men hard. Crusty, dry soil needs a fresh shower of rain to be broken up. The great need is to see the holy, spotless King in His glory, and then you will understand the universality and gravity of sin and the deep need of repentance. It is then that you will fall in love with Him.

A fresh outpouring of the Holy Spirit will produce not only repentance, but it will keep us humble, broken, and softened before Him to whom all things are open and naked (Heb. 4:13).

The true anointing of ministry is what is clearly missing from preachers today. Many are gifted and can dazzle audiences with their charisma and knowledge, but they lack the dew of heaven. Many are like Samson, who did not know that the Spirit of the Lord had departed from him (Jud. 16:20). And just as Samson, we have lost our way.

May God have mercy on us and grant us repentance, and lead us back to the gate of heaven.

CHAPTER 27

SPIRITUAL JUNK FOOD WEAKENING THE CHURCH

"For the time will come when they will not endure sound doctrine, but according to their own desires, because they have itching ears, they will heap up for themselves teachers" (2 Tim. 4:3).

Have you ever asked yourself or quietly wondered why so many in the Western church today lack a strong devotion and dedication to God? Why are there so many professing Christians who still pursue the lusts and pleasures of the world? What kind of conversion experience does someone possess if there is no personal transformation or lifestyle change? These are difficult heart-searching questions that demand answers if we are to see change in our day.

Here are a few other questions to ask ourselves: Why is there such a disparity between Christianity in the Book of Acts and what we are seeing today, especially in the Western world? What caused people in the early Church to sell all their possessions and distribute the proceeds among those who were in need? In the midst of great persecution, what enabled these first-century Christians to continue to serve the Lord fervently? Where did the early apostles and the persecuted Church throughout the ages get the courage and the strength to continue to preach a gospel that was getting them beaten, tortured, and killed, when the biggest struggle for many in the Western church today is the fear of rejection and a need for self-esteem?

I strongly believe that the answer to all these questions and the cure to all the ills that face the Church today are to be found in personal revival in the lives of professing Christians. Without the holy fire of God burning in our hearts through a love relationship with Jesus, we will not be equipped to overcome the complacency, lethargy, and apathy so common in the church world today. We also will not be able to endure the increasing spiritual warfare and antichrist spirit so prevalent in our world. It is the Holy Ghost and the fire of God in our lives that will prepare us for the glory of the Lord and the coming harvest of souls, as well as the Lord's imminent return. The Holy Ghost and fire is how the Church started (Acts 2), and it is how it will end. It is so critical in this dark hour that we burn for Jesus.

A number of years ago, the Lord began dealing with me about writing and speaking on lost themes (see *The Real Spirit of Revival*) — important truths in the body of Christ that have been understated or discarded but that need to be restored.

Some examples of such themes would include the end times, the rapture of the church and the return of the Lord, heaven, hell, and holiness, the Judgment Seat of Christ, etc. He said that there has got to be more preaching on these themes, for they are emphasized in the Holy Scriptures. He also told me that there has been a diabolical silence on holiness that has greatly weakened the character of the Church and opened a door to doctrines of devils.

The absence or dilution of these vital truths has created a large gap between the profession and practice of true Christianity in our day and thus filled our society with much deception. The fear of the Lord, which is the foundation of loving and receiving these truths, is sadly lacking in the church world today.

The emphasis has been on messages for the sweet tooth that take away the offense of the gospel. But have we forgotten that our loving and merciful Savior was called the Rock of Offense?

Pretty words are not always true, and true words are not always pretty.

When someone is used to a light diet or an unhealthy dose of junk food, it will take a little while to adjust to solid, nutritious food again, but that's what the Lord wants for His people in this hour, so that they can be healed and strengthened, and then bear fruit that remains.

May the Lord give you such a love for truth so that you will never again be afraid of a hard word of confrontation and correction. The Lord chastens and corrects those He loves. His love is what gives us value and worth. *"Behold what manner of love the Father has bestowed on us, that we should be called the sons of God!"* (1 John 3:1)

Remember also that God never makes demands of you without empowering you to respond to those demands. He has given us His abounding grace and sent us the Helper, the mighty Holy Spirit, to aid us in every way.

God our Father holds nothing back from us. All that we need to live for Him has been given freely.

"He who did not spare His own Son, but delivered Him up for us all, how shall He not with Him also freely give us all things?" (Rom 8:32).

The word "freely" in this verse is the same root word for "grace." God gives grace. God graciously gives us all things. He equips us to receive His Word and do it. It would be unjust for God to ask us to do something we could not do. This means that what God gives is never the problem. It's what we give Him. The heart and soul of revival is that God wants more of us.

Will you give yourself to Him unreservedly or continue to hold back?

CHAPTER 28

BIBLE BABBLE AND BIBLICAL ILLITERACY

"Jesus answered and said to them, 'You are mistaken (deceived), not knowing the Scriptures nor the power of God'" (Mt. 22:29).

"These were more fair-minded than those in Thessalonica, in that they received the word with all readiness, and searched the Scriptures daily to find out whether these things were so" (Acts 17:11).

Heresy can be fatalistic. Ignorance of the Scriptures engenders bondage. But willful ignorance that leads to Biblical illiteracy is inexcusable. Daily, the Bereans diligently searched the Scriptures to see if what Paul was teaching was true. Today, most Christians easily believe and swallow what the most popular and elevated preachers in our culture say.

The lack of basic Bible knowledge in the church world today is extremely high. Most professing Christians have not read the entire Bible or even the whole of the New Testament once in their lifetime. And some don't want to, which is a bigger problem, symptomatic of the church's backslidings and false conversions. Scripture reading and the necessity for Biblical foundations have been dumbed down, and sadly, some of our pastors are not even qualified to teach the Bible. Moreover, many of our seminaries and Bible colleges generally produce lecturers and theologians void of the Spirit and fire of God, and full of head knowledge that puffs up and spawns unbelief.

Regarding Biblical illiteracy, researchers tell us that it is worse than many have even thought or imagined. Here are some interesting statistics from a recent Barna survey:

- Fewer than half of all adults can name the four gospels.

167

- Many Christians cannot identify more than two or three of the disciples.

- 60 percent of Americans can't name even five of the ten commandments. "Increasingly, America is Biblically illiterate." [see Barna Group's web site]

- According to 82 percent of Americans, "God helps those who help themselves," is a Bible verse. Those identified as born-again Christians did better by only one percent.

- A majority of adults think the Bible teaches that the most important purpose in life is taking care of one's family.

Some of the statistics are rather perplexing even to those aware of the problem.

- One poll indicated that at least 12 percent of adults in America believe that Joan of Arc was Noah's wife.

- Another survey of graduating high school seniors revealed that more than 50 percent thought that Sodom and Gomorrah were husband and wife.

- A considerable number of respondents to one poll indicated that the Sermon on the Mount was preached by Billy Graham.

It would be funny if it wasn't so pathetic.

Perhaps what is even more alarming is that, within churches and organizations that still have a high esteem for Scripture, there is a growing ignorance of the content of Scripture. For many, especially modern-day Charismatics, they regard some inner light or impulse as being "led by the Spirit" or "having a good feeling about it," instead of giving priority of the Spirit's testimony to the written Word. They don't think or study for themselves. I call these Christians modern-day sensationalists who are easily led away by fables and lies, spoken so cleverly by men that they sound like the truth, or they follow teachers who teach in accordance with their own desires.

Not only are ignorance and sensationalism a problem today, but following extreme teachings from Scriptures taken grossly out of context is a major plague in the Charismatic movement. The Bible warns us concerning those who twist Scripture this way:

"Even some men from your own group will rise up and distort the truth in order to draw a following" (Acts 20:30 — NLT).

Charismatics are notorious for pursuing new revelation without the expense of diligent study. And I say this as one who is a strong proponent of the supernatural as you can see from this book. Often, though, we put more stock in ministers who have had visions, visitations, or some other spectacular experience more than the written Word of God. I believe in visions and visitations and all these things, but the Scriptures will forever be our standard.

For example, recently I had a dialogue with a Facebook friend who was posting supposed visions and revelations that people have had of hell, and how many professing Christians were there simply because they had not tithed to their church. When I told him that I couldn't accept the authenticity of these visions based on what Scripture says, he unloaded Bible reference after reference on tithing, in an effort to prove that these visions were from God. But it was all out of context. So it is possible to study the Scriptures diligently but still not rightly divide them and keep them in context when studying a certain topic. This, too, is a common error. If you merely study to prove what you already believe without humility and being teachable, you will miss it.

Knowing that in the last days some will depart from the faith, giving heed to seducing spirits and doctrines of demons should keep us very sober in this regard (1 Tim. 4:1). The anointing of the Holy Spirit does teach us (1 Jn. 2:20, 27) and open our understanding, but we are also commanded to study to show ourselves approved unto God (2 Tim. 2:15). The same Holy Spirit Who leads us and guides us into all truth also inspired the apostle Paul to pronounce a curse on false teachers and those who preached another gospel (1 Gal. 1:8-9).

The biggest problem I've witnessed in almost every movement is the poor use of the full counsel of God. We tend to judge and evaluate everything we believe from our own traditional or denominational perspective or particular stream of faith we might be in.

For instance, the revival camp emphasizes repentance but don't really have a working knowledge of faith. The faith camp emphasizes faith, but many don't understand repentance. The holiness camp emphasizes holy living, but they don't walk in power. The power camp emphasizes signs and wonders, but many of them don't walk in holiness and have faulty foundations in the Word.

The fundamentalists emphasize their strong belief in Scripture but have a reactionary approach to the Bible. They are quick to shout, "If it's not in the Bible, I don't believe it!" but, ironically, they don't believe in tongues and other aspects of the Spirit-filled life. They win people to a doctrine but not to life in Christ. Conversely, the liberals and proponents of the seeker-sensitive philosophy relate to society by compromising truth and softening doctrine to reach the culture, which also creates problems, mainly the lack of true disciples.

When will we learn to reject error and blend all the truths together and be balanced? When will we learn to receive and release the whole counsel of God? (Acts 20:27)

The greatest illiteracy tragedy is concerning the basics of salvation and the Bible. Here are some alarming statistics:

- Out of 79% of evangelicals who say their faith is very important to them, only 36% believe Jesus Christ is actually the only way to salvation. That's a shocker.

- In mainline denominational churches, that percentage drops even more as only 14% believe Jesus Christ is the only way to salvation, while 83% believe all religions lead there.

- Only 22% of mainline denominational churches even believe the Bible is fully inspired by God while 28% believe it is just a book written by men.

- Perhaps the most disturbing trend is among the 18–35 younger group of religious Americans. For many of them Christianity is becoming a watered-down hybrid version of eastern philosophy and biblical knowledge.

While some polls show roughly 9 of 10 Americans still maintain belief in a god or gods, the trend of religious young Americans is toward a conglomeration of varied religious beliefs, including atheism.

This generation must get serious about the problem of Biblical illiteracy, or a frighteningly large number of next-generation Americans — Christians included — will go on thinking that the Bible is really not the inspired Word of God, Jesus is not the only way to salvation, and Noah and his wife Joan of Arc will live happily ever after.

CHAPTER 29

WIMPS AND PIMPS IN THE PULPIT: SPEAK UP OR SHIP OUT

This is an urgent appeal to unmute spineless, yellow-bellied preachers. Can I say it any plainer?

I write as an advocate to those who would like to say certain things to their leader or their pastor, or a host of television preachers but do not have a platform to speak from, or they fear being misunderstood.

Now let me warn you. As you can see by the title of this chapter, this is a very strong and direct word. I have written it with a heavy tone of reproof and rebuke. At first, I thought of softening my words as I read them over and over again, checking my heart all the time I was reading them. Certainly these words do not apply to every preacher, but I sensed the Spirit of God — the same spirit that would come upon the prophets when they would rebuke kings and self-righteous religious leaders. In the end, I decided to leave the chapter as is. In doing so, I know I run the risk of being called harsh, critical, unloving, and judgmental, but I am writing this in the sight of God, and to Him I will give account.

Our nation is under siege. The Supreme Court has made gay marriage a "constitutional right" and federal law. As has been the pattern throughout history in every socialist and communist country, as well as Islamic republics, this law has changed the entire landscape of Christianity in America and will stifle every godly 501C-3 organization, if we let it. The real test of muteness has begun.

How did we get this far? And how will we fare from here? The prophet Jeremiah said it best.

"If you have run with the footmen, and they wearied you, then how can you contend with horses? And if in the land of peace, in which you trusted, they wearied you, then how will you do in the floodplain of the

Jordan?" (Jer. 12:5)

Evil advances when godly men say nothing and do nothing. That is how we've come this far. Not enough pulpits have spoken with fire. Now what will we do if we enter into the floodplain?

I'm grateful for the many godly leaders, ministers, and pastors across this land, but there are still far too many who are riding the fence, being politically correct, playing the part of coexisting cowards, and refusing to speak up on vital issues facing the Church and the nation in this hour.

This is a word for the man-pleasing preacher or pastor who cares more about man's applause than God's approval. This is a tough-loving rebuke for those who are more concerned about their personal popularity and ratings than the power of God and revival.

I do not apologize for speaking bluntly and with candor. If you can't take it, then you may be a wimp.

The dictionary describes a wimp as a weak, ineffectual, and timid person. We have too many of them in our nation's pulpits. The apostle Paul brought correction and encouragement to young Timothy regarding this matter (2 Tim. 1:7). Timothy had become timid during a time of great persecution, but we have become timid in a time when there is little persecution in the West, and relative peace and free speech. Again, as Jeremiah warned, what will we do when in the floodplain?

If you claim to be a preacher and can't stand up for righteousness and speak truth in the midst of such a wicked and perverse generation, you are a wimp.

If you are a pastor and can be easily intimidated into compromise by a controlling elder in your church or a wealthy sponsor of your ministry, then you are a wimp.

If you have surrounded yourself with "yes men" in your organization who court your favor by continually affirming how great you are without ever offering another perspective to any of your decisions, then you are an egotistical wimp.

If your voice can be muted in such a day of gross evil, perversion, and injustice, you are a big wimp.

The real Church doesn't need leaders in their mute and timid state. You are acting the part of a yellow-bellied, lily-livered liability and not an asset. You are aiding the enemy. Our nation's moral crisis calls for preachers now with great courage and conviction. Urgent times require urgent preaching.

As I made reference earlier, there was a day in England when Catherine Booth went from church to church in search of burning words. Her observation had been that there weren't any preachers with fire in their belly. Today it is no different. Many no longer even believe in preaching, but now hold to a conversational style of sermonizing and motivational pep talks. You might be a wimp.

Preaching will never be done away with. Preaching is God's plan, not man's. Quit following the pew and follow God.

And for those of you professing evangelicals and denominational mainline church clergy who believe you can practice homosexuality and follow Jesus at the same time, shame on you! Big shame on you! Preach the Word! You are fighting against God and not man. Put away your limp-wristed humanism and develop some backbone. *"Woe unto you who call evil good, and good evil; who put darkness for light, and light for darkness; who put bitter for sweet, and sweet for bitter"* (Is. 5:20)!

Listen to this scathing statement from the lips of Glen Beck:

"The American Revolution, the Civil War, and the Civil Rights Movement came and were won from the pulpits first. The pulpits should be on fire, but our pulpits are barely an ember! It's shameful what is happening!"

We not only have far too many *wimps* in our pulpits, but we also have an abundance of *pimps* who merchandise and market everything from God's presence to any of His blessings using every kind of trend, fad, and cheap gospel gimmick.

The dictionary defines a pimp as a person, especially a man, who solicits customers for a prostitute or a brothel, usually in return for a share of the earnings.

Pastors, if you treat your congregation like customers, you are a spiritual pimp.

If you are more interested in attendance, buildings, and cash than you are in spiritually preparing your people for the crisis facing our nation and the desperate times we are living in, you may be guilty of pimping them.

If you, as a minister, coerce people into giving a financial offering or a seed in exchange for a 100-fold blessing and what they can get in return, you are a pimp.

Preachers, if you connive the people into thinking that somehow your ministry is the source of the flow of the blessings of God in their lives, you are a pimp.

Every pimp has to gain the trust of his prostitutes. They do this through deception. They don't care about their prostitutes in the same way that these pimping preachers don't care about their audiences.

People of God, don't let pimping preachers make a mockery out of you and deceive you into giving with wrong motivations. The root of their hollow preaching is their greed, their love of money, and their lust for power and influence. They don't really care what God thinks.

Think about it. Where else but in America can a TV minister be convicted of various kinds of scams — from financial embezzlement to tax evasion to infidelity and immoral behavior, only to be right back on TV in the pulpit pimping their audience and selling their best-selling spiritual junk-food books and raking in the big bucks? And the saddest part of it all is that their insensible, adoring fans continue to support them, holding up their God-card of "Thou shalt not judge" for their favorite preacher superstar. What a sham!

Today's Christianity markets everything from "Christian lingerie" to "Christian Exercise videos" to "Anointed Healing Water from the River Jordan" — all for personal gain.

And for those of you holier-than-thou professing evangelical fundamentalists and so-called Pentecostal preachers who complain against American policy that has taken God out of our classrooms and institutions, you cannot speak with any authority because you are guilty of banning the Holy Spirit from speaking and moving in power in your churches, meetings, and classrooms. You suffocate the supernatural with your programs, and you expect to be a spokesman for God against antichrist institutions. Please! If you are going to judge righteously, the first requirement Jesus laid down was for you to remove the plank out of your own eye before attempting to remove the speck in someone else's eye (Mt. 7:1-5).

Pure burning hearts produce flaming tongues, and that is the only kind of preaching that will save America right now.

This quote from Evangelist Mario Murillo says it all:

"If American preaching returns to the Bible and our sermons are thundered from burning hearts full of the Holy Spirit, we have more than a good chance to save America. If preaching stays as is, there is no chance...period. Pastors are dispensing new-age gobbledygook when they should have been training the people in biblical morality. This is one big reason that 6 million Christians voted their pocketbooks instead of their convictions."

Do our nation a favor, preachers. Get some fire in your belly, and preach with some holy conviction.

It may be our last line of hope.

CHAPTER 30

PREACHER AMBIGUITY AND SPEAKING INTO THE AIR

"Even things without life, whether flute or harp, when they make a sound, unless they make a distinction in the sounds, how will it be known what is piped or played? For if the trumpet makes an uncertain sound, who will prepare for battle? So likewise you, unless you utter by the tongue words easy to understand, how will it be known what is spoken? For you will be speaking into the air" (1 Cor. 14:7-9).

Although the subject here is the gift of tongues and interpretation, the point being made is to speak in order to be understood. Too many preachers are not doing that.

GOP candidate and billionaire Donald Trump is teaching preachers a lesson. Many may think he's rude and harsh, but he speaks clearly and plainly and is quite difficult to misunderstand. Most of all, the people are responding to his message.

Perhaps we as preachers have robbed ourselves by being gray instead of black-and-white. Perhaps we've robbed the church of more converts and true followers because we think they don't want to hear plain speech, when, in fact, they do. Perhaps it is time to reconsider that, in our quest not to offend them, we are repelling them.

Ambiguity has no part in the gospel. There is to be a certain and clear sound coming from our pulpits. Political correctness has no part in the ministry of the Lord Jesus Christ. If a preacher cannot speak clearly about the tenets of the faith, especially as it relates to such a sacred subject like marriage (at this time the Supreme Court has ruled in favor of same-sex marriage), he doesn't belong in the pulpit. He needs to get out and find another occupation. A politician might better suit one of such cowardice.

"You be careful when anybody comes to you with a sugar-coated pill

or with a slimy tongue. They are always of the devil. The Spirit of the Lord will always deal with truth." — Smith Wigglesworth

The root of the problem here is money, friends, and influence. Many preachers who are in the limelight will seek to talk in such a way as not to lose money, friends, and influence. Such preachers need to be reminded that our loyalty is not to people but to the truth. I don't care how many favors the people have done for you or how much of a friend they may be. I don't even care if they are close relatives. To prefer them over Jesus and the Scriptures is to be a traitor to the eternal purposes of God.

Both Elijah the prophet and Elisha, his successor, coined this phrase, *"As the Lord God of Israel lives, before whom I stand..."* (1 Kings 17:1, 18:5; 2 Kings 3:14, 5:16). Paul, the apostle, coined a similar expression, *"For we are not, as so many, peddling the word of God; but as of sincerity, but as from God, we speak in the sight of God in Christ"* (2 Cor. 2:17).

In both Elijah's and Paul's day, as it is today, there were many false prophets and apostles who peddled the word of God for money, favor, and influence. However, Elijah and Paul ministered in the sight of God. They were men of sincerity and truth who feared God and hated covetousness. Such were the qualifications for leaders as far back as the time of Moses (Ex. 18:21).

What high-profile religious leaders do when they are faced with a direct question in a public forum is cower down and sugar-coat things they say to avoid offense and controversy. They say it is to keep the door open for the witness of the gospel and not cut off the people they are trying to reach. But when do you tell these people the real, plain, clear truth? The way you win them is ultimately the way you are going to keep them. If you are going to win them with unclear speech and fuzzy doctrine, then you must keep them by feeding them with the same. This is the reason we have so-called "Gay Christians" in our churches. They don't really know where you stand because you've substituted influence for truth.

There is no question we are to love everyone, but there are certain standards in Scripture for membership in a church that professes the Lordship of Jesus Christ.

"For what have I to do with judging those also who are outside? Do you not judge those who are inside? But those who are outside God judges. Therefore 'put away from yourselves the evil person'" (1 Cor. 5:12-13).

In case you didn't know the subject at hand that Paul is addressing, here it is:

"I wrote to you in my epistle not to keep company with sexually immoral people. Yet I certainly did not mean with the sexually immoral people of this world, or with the covetous, or extortioners, or idolaters, since then you would need to go out of the world. But now I have written to you not to keep company with anyone named a brother, who is sexually immoral, or covetous, or an idolater, or a reviler, or a drunkard, or an extortioner — not even to eat with such a person" (1 Cor. 5:9-11).

Paul is addressing habitual sin, especially sexual immorality, in the church. In this case, it was incest. Paul was commanding the Corinthian Christians not to keep company with sexually immoral people who call themselves a brother (or a sister).

Here is a shocker for many: Exclusivity is a part of kingdom culture. Say what? That's right. There is an exclusivity in Christianity. That would include "Gay Christians." Our sympathetic views toward this celebrated group in our culture is a form of cowardice and low esteem for the standards laid out in Scripture. Yes, you will be called hateful and bigoted. But that has been our problem.

We want to blend in with the pop culture instead of stick out. We don't want to be hated or misunderstood. But isn't that also a part of our kingdom culture?

"If the world hates you, you know that it hated Me before it hated you. If you were of the world, the world would love its own. Yet because you are not of the world, but I chose you out of the world, therefore the world hates you" (Jn. 15:18-19).

181

Yet in all this, we are *not* to exclude the world. We are to keep company with them just as our Lord and Master taught us (Lk. 15:1-2). We are to love them and be moved with compassion for them because they are blind (2 Cor.4:3-4).

The issue of habitual sin is a church and kingdom issue, not a world issue. I trust that in attempting to love the sinner — in many cases today, it's the LGBT community — we will find the love and wisdom to do so without compromising the Scriptures.

It's time for a preacher revolution. We need an uprising against the status quo. To regain our ministerial authority, we must swing away from political correctness and stop allowing people's preferences to lead us. We need to return to the roots of Biblical preaching. We need preachers who say what they mean and mean what they say.

Love with truth, compassion with conviction, mercy with might — that is the certain sound that everyone should be hearing.

Anything else is speaking into the air.

CHAPTER 31

THE MAIN DANGER OF THE "HYPER-GRACE" MESSAGE: ERROR THROUGH OVEREMPHASIS

Dietrich Bonhoeffer, the great German pastor and theologian, was asked in 1943 how it was possible for the Church to sit back and let Hitler and the Nazis seize absolute power. Bonhoeffer's reply: *"It was the teaching of cheap grace."*

His firm answer fits the modern day and can greatly aid the Church in narrowing the broad way of destruction, which similar winds of doctrine are paving today. Apparently what he was saying was that the teaching of "cheap grace" resulted in passivity within the Church that greatly diminished human responsibility and allowed the enemy to move in.

What can the Western Church learn from this?

Isn't it interesting that, now, in our day, there are winds of doctrine blowing again which are producing this same type of passive and irresponsible behavior?

With courage and conviction, I must tell you that if a certain course correction is not made with regard to some of these winds of doctrine, it could shipwreck the faith of many professing believers and contribute to the death knell of vibrant Christianity in the West.

The ministry gifts that Jesus gave to the Church (Eph. 4:11) bear the primary responsibility of equipping the saints for works of service so that the body of Christ may reach maturity and will no longer be children tossed to and fro by *"every wind of doctrine."*

"Then we will no longer be immature like children. We won't be tossed and blown about by every wind of new teaching. We will not be influenced when people try to trick us with lies so clever they sound like

the truth" (Eph. 4:14 — NLT).

Winds of doctrine are clever and tricky because there is often truth attached to it. Winds of doctrine are very common when a particular truth is taken out of context or twisted until it actually becomes a lie or is overemphasized at the expense of other equally important truths.

AVOIDING THE DITCHES

Someone once said that if an aircraft leaves New York City with a destination marked for Alaska and the flight course is off by a few degrees upon departure, if not corrected at the offset, it could wind up in Los Angeles. This is the effect that winds of doctrine produce. It is not the 95% truth that will take the body of Christ off course, but the 5% error that will potentially run some into the ditch.

One wise old maestro repeatedly warned his students: *"When it comes to doctrine, stay in the middle of the road, and you will avoid the ditches. Avoid extremes, excesses, and abuses of doctrine."*

This is what I've witnessed regarding what many refer to as the "hyper-grace" message — many truths overemphasized at the expense of other equally important truths. These so-called "new" truths are not new, nor are they "revolutionary," as some say. They come around about every 20 to 25 years or once every generation.

The message of what Bonhoeffer called "cheap grace" was around in the 1930s and '40s. Finis Dake called it "ultra-grace." Today it's called "hyper-grace." These winds of doctrine toss immature believers to and fro through overemphasis or clever lies that sound like the truth. Sadly, even preachers sometimes get caught up in these winds. It is a characteristic of immaturity.

Here's an example from a book of one of the leading proponents of "hyper-grace."

In this book he compares what he calls the "mixed-grace" message with the "hyper-grace" message.

- Mixed-grace is grace + effort; you're saved by grace and kept by works.

- Hyper-grace is grace alone; you're saved by grace and kept by grace.

Now, what is wrong with that comparison? There is actually truth in both statements, but because the book is emphasizing the hyper-grace message, it de-emphasizes the other perspective. Here he rightfully declares that we are saved and kept by grace, while minimizing the importance of effort and works. The Scriptures, however, have so much to say concerning the importance of our works, the truth of it being so obvious, that it is ridiculous and an insult to true Christian intelligence to elaborate on it in any great depth here.

It is like asking, "Does obedience save you or keep you saved?" Yes and no. We're saved by grace through faith, but faith without works is dead. Actually, imbalances constantly occur when we isolate certain Scriptures at the expense of the sum counsel of the Word.

For example, by isolating the following Scriptures, we could conclude that we are indeed saved by works and obedience.

*"You see then that a man is justified by **works,** and not by faith only"* (Jam. 2:24).

*"And we are His witnesses to these things, and so also is the Holy Spirit whom God has given to those who **obey Him**"* (Acts 5:32).

*"And having been perfected, He became the author of eternal salvation to all who **obey Him**"* (Heb. 5:9).

But the middle-of-the-road truth is that works and obedience are outflows of an inward grace and faith. They are evidence of our salvation.

Here's another one of his comparisons:

- Mixed-grace says forgiveness is maintained through repentance and confession.

- Hyper-grace says forgiveness is a done deal; in Christ, we are *eternally* forgiven.

Once again, there is truth on both sides, but the error arises from overemphasizing one at the expense of the other. The aircraft is off course by 5 degrees in both statements.

For example, if all a believer does is repent and confess his sins and never learns to stand on God's grace and Christ's righteousness, he will have a tendency to develop a guilt-consciousness and will never be able to take full advantage of his position in Christ.

On the other hand, if forgiveness is a done deal, and we are *eternally* forgiven for our past, present, and even future sins, then repentance and confession become unnecessary. Over the course of time, you can readily see where that will lead you. Soon, every carnal man would be doing what is right in his own eyes, and spiritual anarchy would ensue.

Here's one more:

- Mixed-grace tells us to be holy because, without holiness, no one will see the Lord — so watch yourself.

- Hyper-grace says, "In Christ you are holy — so be who you truly are."

Again, there are truths in both statements, but the mixed-grace message insinuates that it is wrong to "watch yourself." But the Bible admonishes us to watch ourselves.

Examine yourself (2 Cor. 13:5).

Judge yourself (1 Cor. 11:28-31).

Take heed to yourself (1 Tim. 4:14).

Cleanse yourself (2 Cor. 7:1).

Although some of the truths of the hyper-grace message are actually sound positional truths, the error through overemphasizing one and minimizing the other creates an imbalance that is potentially dangerous.

Here's the problem:

The "hyper-grace" message emphasizes the God-side of redemption while nearly refuting and dismissing the man-side. It rightly brings emphases to what God has wrought in us through the grace of God in Christ, but it de-emphasizes the human side and responsibility of walking it out.

The Bible is a mixture of positional truths and the practical application of those truths. We need both. The apostle Paul tells us to put off the old man's deeds and put on the new man. He exalts the finished work of Christ in the heavenlies, but he also instructs us on how to practically live out that truth in our earthly walk.

Why do you suppose Paul gave that kind of instruction to born-again, Spirit-filled people if it was just supposed to happen automatically? And the other New Testament writers followed the same pattern, often reminding these early saints not to sin, lie, steal, commit adultery and fornication, to make their calling and election sure, to maintain good works, etc. The epistles are full of such admonitions.

Even though God, through His grace, was working in the believer to will and to do of His good pleasure, Paul reminded them to work out their salvation with fear and trembling (Phil. 2:12-13).

What some advocates of hyper-grace call the mixed-grace message is simply the God-side and man-side of our redemption and sanctification.

SANCTIFY YOURSELF

It is true that God has already sanctified us. It is true that Jesus Christ is our sanctification (1 Cor. 1:30). That is a high and lofty positional truth expounding on the legal aspect of our sanctification. But the Word also tells us to sanctify ourselves and reminds believers of their personal responsibility to apply that sanctification to their lives. That is called the vital or the experiential aspect of our redemption and sanctification.

So in essence, what I've observed in the "hyper-grace" teaching is error through simple overemphasis of one glorious truth at the expense of an almost complete dismissal of another equally important truth. We need the mixture of the God-side and the man-side of our sanctification.

Paul was sanctified and separated from his mother's womb (Gal. 1:15), but he also sanctified himself lest he be disqualified (1 Cor. 9:24-27). The imagery in these verses is that of a Grecian Olympic athlete who trained rigorously for 10 months to compete in the games. That doesn't sound too effortless to me, and yet when we yield to the inward grace, it seems effortless. That is the balance.

Because Paul sanctified himself, he admonished Timothy to do the same (2 Tim. 2:21-22). *"Purge yourself"* is a part of the language Paul uses — yet another example of the man-side of our sanctification. The problem has been that we are asking God to do many things for us which He tells us to do ourselves.

Of course, He supplies the grace and the Holy Spirit to help us, but He will not do it for us. The Holy Spirit is a Helper, not a doer. There are perhaps hundreds of examples in the New Testament of this sort of cooperation that exists between God and man, and between grace and works.

I think it's high time in the body of Christ to heed the wise old maestro's sound wisdom: "Avoid the ditches, and stay in the middle of the road."

In doing this, you will not be tossed by winds of doctrine, and the grace of God won't be received in vain (2 Cor. 6:1).

CHAPTER 32

THE INCLUSIVITY AND EXCLUSIVITY OF TRUE CHRISTIANITY: A KEY REASON WHY THERE IS SO MUCH UNCHECKED SIN IN THE CHURCH

The gospel is for everyone. All sinners are welcome — liars, thieves, whoremongers, prostitutes, murderers, homosexuals, drunkards, and drug addicts. The poor, the downtrodden, the broken-hearted, the outcast, and the rejects of society are all welcome.

The gospel is also for those who appear sweet and nice but are full of inward vice. And let's not forget self-righteous religious citizens, who also outwardly appear beautiful but are spiritually dead in their trespasses and sins — they, too need salvation. The gospel is also for the professional people such as doctors, lawyers, and successful businesspeople who seem to have it all together but inwardly are full of dead men's bones. All have sinned and come short of the glory of God (Rom. 3:23).

The gospel of Jesus Christ excludes no one and puts a higher value on humanity than any other religion ever known to mankind.

But once a sinner is saved and becomes a member of the body of Christ in a local church, the fellowship is no longer all inclusive. There was a certain standard established by the early apostles to remain a part of the Christian fellowship. Anyone *practicing* a lifestyle of sin was to be avoided and rejected, but only after relational steps had been taken in an attempt to bring them to repentance and restoration (Mat. 18:15-17).

Immoral persons were not permitted in the fellowship (1 Cor. 5:9) — nor were those who were unruly and walked disorderly (2 Thes. 3:6). Domineering and sectarian leaders were excluded (3 John 9-11). Those who defiled their separation from the world were excommunicated (Rev. 3:15-16). Fellowship was also based on believing and receiving the doctrine of Christ (2 John 9-11).

Today this sort of divine discipline is clearly missing from church practice. Many don't understand the ramifications of its neglect or how to employ it. Yet, in the early days of the Church, it was used to preserve the purity and unity of the body of Christ. It was enforced by mature, authorized ministers and a church filled with the love of God who had a singular eye toward the glory of God. Also, it was exercised only when other means had been exhausted, and such cases were rare.

Nevertheless, beginning with the first case of Ananias and Sapphira, when divine discipline was exercised, we see a great fear coming on the Church that brought a halt to any such sinful behavior or serious misconduct in others (Acts 5:1-11). When believers recognize the supernatural element in divine authority, they will not be so reckless and irresponsible in their behavior. Granted, the number of cases where this sort of divine judgment was exercised was small, but it was used as a means to purify the Church and preserve its unity.

Believers who would hastily pronounce divine judgment on others should be warned against the danger of using any gift of God for vengeance or vindication. Unfair or unjust discipline that is applied for selfish reasons is contrary to the will of God and will not work. The Church is imperfect, and there will always be immaturity and carnality manifested among the saints. However, when a serious situation arises that threatens the purity and unity of the local church, immediate action should be taken.

"Assuredly, I say to you, whatever you bind on earth will be bound in heaven, and whatever you loose on earth will be loosed in heaven" (Mat 18:18).

In such serious cases as the man in 1 Cor. 5 who was committing incest with his stepmother, or the two men, Hymenaeus and Philetus, who denied the resurrection and were overthrowing the faith of some (2 Tim. 2:17-18), God has given the church supernatural authority to bind and loose and to keep the church free of desecration.

Could the absence of this type of divine discipline in the Church today be the reason she is so divided and defiled, and commands so little respect from the world? Could the reason this discipline is not being applied when necessary also be due to the shortage of godly, mature leadership in the church?

I propose we look at what Scripture says on this important topic with fresh, new eyes and a teachable spirit that is ready to receive the Holy Spirit's enlightenment.

CHAPTER 33

BE CAREFUL WHO YOU CALL A HERETIC

I have frequently observed many professing Christians lash out and criticize ministers by name whom they do not know personally or have no sure witness of the things they accuse them of. I am especially grieved by the hearts of some who insist on calling certain ministers heretics.

Do we realize what a serious charge it is to call a minister of the gospel a heretic? In order to make this accusation you better have done your homework and got your facts straight. If not, you are on dangerous ground with God. Publicly calling someone a heretic who is not a heretic is slander and defamation of character, and simply a lack of Christian integrity.

Some have even gone further with their accusations and refuse to call any of these men brothers or even ministers whom God has called.

So the question we must ask is: What constitutes heresy?

Let's begin by identifying what does *not* constitute heresy. Paul, speaking in 1 Cor. 13 on divine love, said, *"For now we see through a glass darkly; but then face to face: now we know in part; but then shall I know even as also I am known"* (1 Cor. 13:12).

It appears from this statement that perfect doctrinal agreement and unity shall never be achieved on this side of heaven. Any attempts to do so will engender much contention and strife. Even ministers of the same denomination often disagree over certain matters of doctrine. Also, in the course of a lifetime, Christians and ministers will modify their views and beliefs many times as they receive more light and understanding from the Scriptures. Our fellowship with one another should never be based on conformity to all details of doctrine but must be based more on the melding of our hearts together in love by the Spirit of God.

It is more important to maintain unity in the body of Christ than to resolve petty doctrinal differences.

The only doctrinal agreement we must have as Christians and ministers is on the principles of the doctrine of Christ (Heb. 6:1-2). These are the fundamentals of the foundation of our faith, without which we cannot have any fellowship. Here are the six principles:

1. Repentance from dead works

2. Faith toward God

3. Doctrine of baptisms

4. Laying on of hands

5. Resurrection of the dead

6. Eternal judgment

The basis for fellowship and dis-fellowship in the body of Christ concerning doctrine is based on these six principles, as John the apostle states.

"He that abides in the doctrine of Christ, he has both the Father and the Son. If there come any unto you, and bring not this doctrine, receive him not into your house, neither bid him God speed" (2 John 9:10).

Now to be ignorant of these essentials of the Christian faith is one thing, but to turn away from them, or to preach contrary to them after having knowledge of them, is quite another. There are several examples in Scripture of men perverting these principles. For example, Paul writes about two men who perverted the doctrine of the resurrection, causing some people's faith to be overthrown.

"And their message will spread like cancer. Hymenaeus and Philetus are of this sort, who have strayed concerning the truth, saying that the resurrection is already past; and they overthrow the faith of some" (2 Tim. 2:17-18).

Individual Christians and especially ministers who deny the truth of the resurrection are to be denied fellowship, but only after being confronted and warned.

"Having faith and a good conscience, which some having rejected, concerning the faith, have suffered shipwreck, of whom are Hymenaeus and Alexander, whom I delivered to Satan that they may learn not to blaspheme" (1 Tim 1:20).

Paul turned these two men over to Satan for blaspheming. It appears that these were the same men who were perverting the doctrine of the resurrection.

A heretic is a person who perverts the doctrine of Christ in one of these six principles. As a modern-day example, there are ministers now who are teaching universalism, which is to say that everyone will one day be saved. I know of at least one of these men who used to be one of my favorite preachers when I was in Bible school. He was a strong repentance-and-revival preacher who emphasized holiness. Now he fellowships with every kind of religion and says that every one of them will be saved. I know of ministers who no longer believe in a literal hell and write books to discredit it. These are examples of the perversion of eternal judgment. These are ministers who started out right but became apostate and, sadly, left the doctrine of Christ.

Someone close to them in a position of ministerial authority should have confronted these men in love and gone through the proper relational steps to restore them (Mat. 18:15-17). I say this with fear and trembling, but if these heretics refused to listen, then they should've been turned over to Satan, so that repentance may work in them, and their soul might yet be restored.

Remember, heresy has nothing to do with a person's wealth and possessions; it has nothing to do with his personality or success, or the fact he doesn't preach a strong repentance message, or that he cowered down in a national television interview and refused to call sin, sin.

Heresy is not teaching financial prosperity and God's will to prosper and bless His children. It's not believing and teaching on the pre-tribulation rapture versus post-tribulation. A minister is not a heretic because he performs miracles in the name of Jesus, while lacking the fruit of the spirit in his life. Power and fruit are two different things. Paul told the Corinthians that they came behind in no gift and yet called them carnal (1 Cor. 1:7; 3:3). None of these constitute a perversion of the doctrine of Christ. None of these constitute heresy. So I ask you again, under what grounds of evidence have you the right to call any of these men heretics?

Now, I realize that, when ministers leave certain components of the gospel and important Scriptural truths out of their preaching, it can open a large door for the sinner and the halfhearted to feel comfortable in their sins and in their worldly lifestyle. And when that becomes the norm or status quo in a church, it can cultivate an atmosphere of deception. When it comes to even the basic message of salvation, I realize many are being errantly taught that all you need to do is to acknowledge your belief in Jesus, say a little prayer, and you're in. Nothing is ever said before or after salvation about true heart-repentance, surrendering your life — losing it to gain it, following Jesus in wholehearted obedience, and loving Him above all others.

Now if this is the beef that you have against any of today's ministers, that still does not make them a heretic, or a wolf, or an agent of Satan (some actually believe that about these ministers). It could just mean that they minister a light spiritual diet with some junk food mixed in. Instead of serving up meat and potatoes, green beans, Brussel sprouts, and spinach, they serve a large dose of cookies, cake, and ice cream with a glass of milk.

But that still doesn't make them heretics.

CHAPTER 34

SPIRITUAL ADULTERY AND FORNICATION

Just a few decades ago, it was easier to tell the difference between a real Christian and a non-Christian, a saint and a sinner. There was not the kind of wiggle room we have today when we say of some professing Christian, "He's a Christian, but he's really messed up on drugs." Or "He's got a good heart, but he lives with his girlfriend." Or nowadays, "She believes in Jesus, but she's gay."

Certainly when a person is truly converted, he does not become perfect or completely sanctified overnight, but at some early point in his Christian walk, any genuine believer should be showing evidence and fruit of a true conversion. A grace that does not change us is not the grace of God.

Not only is the church vastly different than it was a few decades ago, but it is such a phantom of the original copy in its earliest beginnings that it would be difficult for the early apostles to recognize it. Except in a few nations of the world where there is great persecution, and in some obscure places, it is becoming increasingly difficult to recognize the spirit and the message of today's Christianity.

Back in the days of the early Church, being in ministry leadership was the greatest sacrifice anyone could make, and it reflected the message of the greatest sacrifice that was made — the cross. To be in ministry leadership today can be as easy as ordering an ordination certificate through the mail, taking a few Bible courses, polishing up your sermon presentations, learning some leadership and church-growth principles, including how to win friends and influence people, and you're in. I know this sounds a little sarcastic, but the point is made, nonetheless.

In the early Church's purest form, the cross was the power of God and the center of Christianity, ruling the lives of the early believers. They had as their examples apostolic men who apprenticed under Jesus and who hazarded their lives for the sake of the gospel. There was no mistaking the pattern and the purpose of the lives of those first-day apostles. It is the reason they had power to make radical disciples who were distinct from the world. What they preached and what they practiced enabled them to transform the minds and hearts of so many. We have so little power to transform people's lives today because we do not preach and live the cross.

The cross is not just about Jesus Christ dying for the sins of all mankind, but it was a death to purchase mankind. We were bought by His precious blood (1 Cor. 6:20) (1 Pet. 1:18-19). The cross is symbolic of our own death and separation from the world. Christians are people who are *in* the world but not *of* it. They do not partake of the carnal amusements and follies of the world that compromise their separation. They are not addicted to entertainment, obsessed with sports, caught up in worldly fashion, and indulging their lives on the flesh.

The Word of God likens the Church to a chaste virgin that is presented to Christ (2 Cor. 11:2). Defilement of this separation is called spiritual adultery and fornication.

"Adulterers and adulteresses! Do you not know that friendship with the world is enmity with God? Whoever therefore wants to be a friend of the world makes himself an enemy of God" (Jam. 4:4).

Who is your friend? And who is your enemy?

In the church of Thyatira, a false prophetess named Jezebel was apparently causing many in the church to defile themselves by spiritual fornication. The Lord severely rebuked the church for allowing this condition to continue.

"Nevertheless I have a few things against you, because you allow that woman Jezebel, who calls herself a prophetess, to teach and seduce My servants to commit sexual immorality and eat things sacrificed to idols" (Rev. 2:20-22).

History also offers us the possibility that this could've been physical fornication. Ancient types of labor unions called guilds controlled all commerce in Thyatira. The city was famous for the common practice of sealing business contracts by making an offering to a god in a temple and then having sex with a temple prostitute to seal the deal. Either way, whether spiritual or carnal fornication, it was causing Christians to compromise their separation from the world.

Another factor which contributed to the defilement of early Christians occurred sometime toward the end of Paul's life and years before John died. This was the time a philosophy called Gnosticism arose. It taught Christians that the body is inherently sinful and evil but that the spirit is born again and pure and holy. Therefore, one could live how they pleased in this life, because, in your spirit, you were righteous and heaven-bound. This sounds uncannily similar to some extreme teachings today.

This doctrine of Gnosticism gave professing Christians justification to live like the world while remaining a "Christian." It also kept them from being martyred for their faith if they wanted out. This heresy greatly threatened to dilute the message and ministry of the cross.

Over time, this belief system meant people could be "believers" in Jesus or "fans" of Jesus without actually being *disciples* of Jesus and answering the call to be separate from the world. As I said, we are seeing this today in various forms of philosophies and teachings.

John also addressed this demonic doctrine of Gnosticism that could lead to spiritual adultery and fornication, and he admonished Christians not to love the world.

"Do not love the world or the things in the world. If anyone loves the world, the love of the Father is not in him. For all that is in the world— the lust of the flesh, the lust of the eyes, and the pride of life — is not of the Father but is of the world" (1 John 2:15-17).

Lest any professing Christian take this lightly or throw this off as some legalistic form of doctrine or a turning back to the law, let me remind you that Jesus called it "the depths of Satan."

"Now to you I say, and to the rest in Thyatira, as many as do not have this doctrine, who have not known <u>the depths of Satan</u>, as they say, I will put on you no other burden. But hold fast what you have till I come" (Rev. 2:24-25).

One translation says that the false teachers of John's day called this doctrine of Gnosticism, which permitted spiritual adultery and fornication, thus defiling the Christian's separation from the world, *"the deeper truths of Christianity."* What some were calling *"deeper truths,"* Jesus said were *"the depths of Satan."* Things haven't changed too much in this regard from what we are seeing in our modern day.

We've got to recover the spirit and the message of true Christianity. God is working to restore to the Church its true character, power, and authority. Without the preaching and practice of the life of the cross, we won't get there.

Beware of a cross-less Christianity which breeds spiritual adultery and fornication.

PART III

PROJECT STEPHEN: A PORTRAIT OF A LAST DAYS PREACHER

CHAPTER 35

A MANIFESTO FOR A NEW BREED

"Your young men shall see visions..." (Acts 2:17).

"But he (Stephen), being full of the Holy Spirit, gazed into heaven and saw the glory of God, and Jesus standing at the right hand of God, and said, 'Look! I see the heavens opened and the Son of Man standing at the right hand of God!' Then they cried out with a loud voice, stopped their ears, and ran at him with one accord; and they cast him out of the city and stoned him. And the witnesses laid down their clothes at the feet of a young man named Saul" (Acts 7:55-58).

Stephen was a young man of good reputation, full of the Holy Spirit, faith, and wisdom. Most of us would be thrilled to be noted for just one or two of these godly qualities. As we will soon discover, Stephen possessed not only these but would be given more.

Stephen was a holy vessel of a wholly new order effecting disorder among the self-righteous crowd. He was fit for the Master's use but unfit for the religious system of his day. God raised him up in a blaze of great persecution. Stephen answered the call and sealed his fiery message with his own blood.

Will there be end-time persecution in America as great as that which was in Jerusalem long ago? And will there again be Stephens among us who have grand visions of heaven and of the glory of God? And will some be killed for telling the truth?

We have reason to believe that Stephen's forgiveness of his accusers and murderers was instrumental in bringing forth new birth in another young man named Saul. As Stephen's life and earthly destiny ended with visions of heaven, so Saul's new life would soon begin with the same. And as Stephen suffered this great persecution, so Saul would suffer much more.

Saul became Paul because Stephen cried out for his forgiveness. The witnesses at his death laid down their clothes at Saul's feet, but it was Stephen's loud praying that would later lay down new paths for those same feet.

Stephen's violent departure led to Saul's violent entry into the kingdom of God. Will this kind of violence be more frequent and mark these last days? Where are the voices of the spiritually violent witnesses, pray-ers, and preachers that are producing violent conversions?

Besides the blameless character of this young man, Stephen, there are three more radical qualities which distinguish him from most modern-day preachers. I believe these qualities to be the stamp of a true warrior and a new breed of revivalist that will prepare the way for the Lord's impending return. Here they are:

1. His message was irresistible.

"And they were not able to resist the wisdom and the spirit by which he spake" (Acts 6:10).

2. His miracles were great and done "among" the people.

"And Stephen, full of faith and power, did great wonders and miracles among the people" (Acts 6:8).

3. His martyrdom was the embodiment of the love of our Savior and came with visions of heaven.

"And they stoned Stephen, calling upon God, and saying, 'Lord Jesus, receive my spirit'" (Acts 7:59).

Can there be any greater heaven-demanding and hell-busting qualities than these? They convey both alarm and assault to Satan and his demons. They cause quaking and trembling in his darkest regions, and glory and rejoicing in the highest of heavens.

Ministry gifts must be unwrapped through prayer. Birth must be given to a new breed of preachers on the earth in this final hour.

I believe that the coming apostolic ministries of our day will be carriers of true revival. Like Stephen of old, they will be full of faith and power and do great wonders and signs among the people, while speaking with an irresistible wisdom and Spirit. They will not count their lives dear to themselves but instead will be utterly abandoned to God's eternal purposes.

The combination of the deeply convicting repentance preaching of one like Charles Finney and the daring, miracle-working faith of one like Smith Wigglesworth will bring a mighty apostolic anointing and authority that has been lacking in recent times. It will ignite the common man to carry that witness into the marketplace.

CHAPTER 36

THE MESSAGE: IRRESISTIBLE WISDOM

Our modern gospel is a bark at best. Stephen's words cut to the heart (Acts 7:54), causing a rage and a fury in those who opposed it.

"Such preaching, by making indifference impossible, set hearers in one of two camps. It is calculated to produce a revival or a riot." (Arthur Wallis on Apostolic Preaching).

On the day of Stephen's lofty discourse, no conversions were recorded, but as we've already seen, Saul's subsequent conversion was a result of Stephen's stoning. And we all know how the Lord used Saul to change the course of history.

No conversions were recorded, but the hearers were smitten. Today they are massaged and put to sleep instead of being violently awakened.

On an individual level, I have witnessed the biting effect the gospel can have on its hearers. One time a pastor and his wife sat with my wife and me at a restaurant. It was soon evident that this restaurant's waiters were homosexuals and perhaps hired by gay management. Now homosexuality is a sin like any other sin from which there can be freedom and deliverance, but it is unnatural and grievous to the Lord. People must be told in love and kindness that it is wrong.

God loves every sinner without approving of their sin. We've majored on God's love and acceptance without even mentioning His disapproval. A false comfort has hardened sinners to the real gospel. Their sin and evil has not been exposed because we've catered to their rebellion and pride all in the name of love.

Before a patient can appreciate and receive a cure, he must know he is sick. I'm using this example of homosexuality because of its wide acceptance in Western culture. Not only is it tolerated, but now it is celebrated.

At any rate, here we are sitting at this restaurant, being served by homosexuals. After being asked and responding affirmatively to his belief in the Bible, I told our waiter what the Scriptures said of the sin of homosexuality. *"It is an abomination to God"* (Lev. 18:22), I said. Little did I know or expect what the confrontation of this sin would bring in that restaurant.

Apparently this message was passed on to other waiters because it seemed like, one by one, some of them would pass by our table and give us the evil eye. What a commotion my words caused! Their secure stronghold was being shaken. Their comfortable lifestyle was being afflicted. Their private sin was being brought to light. Demons were mad. Their fury was reflected on these young men. The gospel had bitten them.

Before leaving this restaurant, we wrote a kind note to this waiter, with a large gratuity attached to it. We let him know of our genuine love and concern for his soul. The gospel was sown. We walked away in peace, having also learned the value and effect of using the Law to reveal the knowledge of sin (Rom. 3:20).

Granted, you will not always deal with every sinner the same way. Jesus certainly didn't. We must follow the leading of the Holy Spirit. But, in this particular case, it was what the Spirit called for.

It can be very painful for a doctor to tell a patient of their terminal illness. Imagine this scenario: A person is diagnosed with a rare, quickly spreading cancer. To numb the pain and attack the cancer cells, the doctor prescribes two kinds of very strong medication, but he doesn't know how to break the tragic news of the life-threatening disease to the patient.

There is only a small chance of recovery if the medication continues to be taken regularly and in large doses. The doctor emphasizes the importance of the medication to the patient, but he speaks of the disease only in general terms, without specifically revealing its terminal effects. Therefore, not knowing the seriousness of the disease and the consequences of neglecting the medication, the patient is not faithful in administering the doctor's prescribed doses, and so he dies.

The physical pain was bad enough, so the doctor refused to burden the patient with the emotional trauma of knowing the terminal possibilities of the disease. His intent was to comfort the patient, but, instead, he killed him.

A false comfort prevented the patient from embracing the medication. This may not be the perfect example, but it illustrates what we've done with our modern gospel message. I understand perfectly that the letter of the Law kills, but a false comfort is just as deadly. If sinners are going to esteem Jesus Christ, they've got to know the cause and consequences of their sin. They've got to understand that all sinners, until they come to repentance and faith, are under the wrath of God (John 3:36).

The patient didn't know how sick he was. Sin is exceedingly sinful (Rom. 7:13). The punishment for sin is exceedingly severe (eternity in hell). Why aren't we telling them?

Years ago, I was given an opportunity to speak to approximately 150 poor and homeless folks. These were not proud homosexuals but a downtrodden people. The situation and circumstances of these people called for a different approach. God gave me a message for the broken-hearted and grace for their grief, but it still came with fire — and some were stung.

Just as I was preparing to give the altar call, a female Elymas (the sorcerer, Acts 13:8) flung her arms in the air and ordered the meeting stopped. Conviction was upon many, and the gifts of the Holy Spirit were crackling in my belly. I was ready to call out certain physical needs for healing, but the authorities who invited me made the decision to bring the whole thing to a halt.

I couldn't entirely blame our gracious hosts because they were also subject to the authorities of the facility being used for this outreach.

Nevertheless, I was wounded and grieved. Jealousy for the Lord's honor filled my heart. I saw it as a victory for the devil and a loss for the kingdom of God. I still thanked God that the incorruptible Word was sown.

Where did we ever get this idea that, if the gospel is presented in the right way, it will never offend? Is a light gospel better than a hard gospel? Do we want 100 false converts or 10 true ones? Are we better than Jesus and the apostles? Are we wiser than Stephen?

Wherever the true gospel is preached in the power of the Spirit, the hearers will either be bitten and smitten, or they will be bitten and stiffen. If people are not moved one way or the other, the preacher has done a bad job.

In this case, one person influenced by the biggest stiff — Satan closed down an altar call. If it had been my meeting alone, I would've challenged Elymas and, with God's help, won. This flagrant opposition was not to be recognized as a careless distraction, but a demon-designed attack on the anointing of the Holy Spirit.

Like a pesky hornet, the true message of the gospel will sting demons; like a sharp knife, it will cut at the fleshly nature of man; and, like a two-edged sword, it will probe and penetrate the conscience.

There was a seasoned wisdom in young Stephen, however. He began his fiery message with a slow burn. He found a place where his hearers, those Law-breaking Jews, could agree with him and his message. Stephen rehashed Jewish history from the Old Testament, something all true Jews were familiar with. Beginning with Abraham and the patriarchs, Stephen weaved through God's dealings with Israel before finally ending with a sharp rebuke.

By this anointing, Stephen whetted the appetite of his Jewish brethren and made the message tasteful and appealing until the end, when he drove that gospel dagger into their hearts.

Oh, for a new breed of tender, fire-hearted preachers who refuse to *soothe* and instead choose to *scorch* seared consciences! Oh, for a modern-day Finney and a Spurgeon who will not *smile* on sin but *slap* it; who will not only *scrape* their idols but *smash* them, and with wit and wisdom from God will win the humble and broken to Christ!

CHAPTER 37

THE MIRACLES: MANTLES OF MIGHT

Demons entice sinners by entertaining them with the sweet bait of lustful play and sinful pleasure. The bland and the boring are identified with God, while the dainty and delightful are unknowingly credited to Satan. The master of deception has succeeded in distracting the multitudes.

Secular artists are in alliance with evil to accomplish hell's top mission: Activate and accelerate the minds of the masses and make them too busy to stop, too unsettled to stand, too noisy to hear, and too numb to feel the conviction of the Spirit.

Hell's carefully planned distractions are always designed to keep the multitudes free from viewing and knowing Christ, the main attraction. Hell's fulfillment of this, their highest purpose, can be halted only when a sinner's mind is assaulted, and his heart attacked by the Spirit's thunderous blast.

Mighty miracles point the barrel of the gun at the sinner's back and declare: "Stop. Stand still. Don't move. Put your hands on your head. You're under arrest." Now his rights can be read, and he can be guided and led to repair and repent.

Where are the sharp-shooting gunmen whose wonders place people under arrest and whose words do more than just caress? Where are the feared miracle ministries and marshals?

Philip was one of those miracle marshals and sharpshooters from out west. He traveled east to Samaria, looking for criminals to arrest. Philip's miracles arrested, and his message was convincing and uncontested.

Try to imagine a place like Samaria. This wicked city was

213

completely under the rule of sorcery whose main operation came through one man. These Samarians were astonished at this man's magical powers, and they listened to him. His false miracles produced a false arrest of an entire city. The inhabitants exclaimed this sorcerer as the great power of God.

This ruling principality and power of sorcery had occupied this city for a long time. It would take real Holy Ghost muscle to move this territorial tycoon out of Samaria.

When a man and a ministry of miracles come to an occupied demonic territory, he comes immaculately dressed with an armor of authority that reflects the know-so confidence he possesses. He knows when Christ comes to a city, he doesn't come to compromise or negotiate. There are no terms for any sort of agreement.

In the Old Testament, Israel's enemies would either surrender and live or oppose and die. Satan's power is no match for God. Under a miracle ministry, his weapons of deception are brought to naught every single time.

To be harassed and embarrassed by already-defeated demon power only means you are the one who's deceived. Like Pharaoh's magicians challenged Moses, Satan may challenge a man or a ministry who show any bit of hesitation and doubt. *But a man with a mantle — and a ministry with a mandate — Satan can never intimidate.*

Let me show you what I mean. Musa is an African from a church I often minister in. A number of years ago, God opened a door for Musa to visit and witness to Mohammed Ali, the former boxer. At the time of this amazing encounter, Ali was no longer a man who "floats like a butterfly and stings like a bee." He was a very sick and demonized man. Musa met with him in a hotel suite.

For a man of Ali's status to welcome an unknown into the privacy of his hotel room was an obvious sign of the Lord's favor. After making his intentions of sharing the gospel with Ali clearly known, Ali invited Musa to sit beside him.

Reaching for his briefcase, Ali pulled out a Bible and, with cockeyed confidence, made his boast to Musa of having read the Bible through 22 times. Then he proceeded to let Musa know of the many contradictions he found therein. But Musa softly reasoned that his visit's purpose was not to argue or debate scripture.

Then something eerie happened. Ali must have thought, "If Musa won't be impressed with my knowledge, then I'll dazzle him with something else." With this thought, Ali arose from his sitting position, and yielding to strong magical powers, began to levitate his large body off the floor and into the air.

And then with a hellish pride and demon glee, he looked at Musa and asked him, "Can your God do this?"

Now if you had been placed in Musa's predicament, what would you have done? Here's what Musa did.

As Ali yielded to his god, so now Musa gave way to his. Without even thinking, Musa yielded his spirit and tongue to God's authority, and with a loud voice, commanded that demon of levitation to loose Ali's body. And with that rebuke, Ali's body came crashing and crumpling to the floor. Glory to God! Our Christ will never be outmatched, outdone, or shown up by any form of demon power.

Well, the battle between Ali's god and Musa's God was not yet over, as we will soon see. Ali and the demons that controlled him were upset, to say the least. With a mad, dashing burst of energy, Ali came off the floor and began to go after Musa. He chased him around the room, but using a round table for protection, Musa pled the blood of Jesus against Ali's unholy rage.

Finally, the demons weakened and whimpered. Tired and whipped, their agent Ali sat harmlessly gazing at a Holy Ghost-filled man who met his challenge. Then with an uncertain look in his eyes, Ali conceded to defeat and directed these confirming words to Musa: "I've challenged many ministers with my power, and not one has contested me. But you are different! You really believe, don't you?"

Do we, like Musa, *really believe?*

A man with an assignment will not be subject to confinement. He knows Satan has been stripped and spoiled of all his power. Satan lost. Christ is boss.

That is why a humble man imbued with this knowledge and power can appear bossy. He cannot afford to be anything less than that. His very attitude speaks.

When he steps up to the plate, he points to the grandstands, *a la* Babe Ruth. Such a man knows the score. He comes to town with might and miracles to hit a home run.

"Win. Conquer. Take over. That is the language of miracles."

Demons were cast out under Philip's anointed proclamation and power. Christ's authority in Philip made demons cry. Today, they often sigh. They're relieved because there are so few with divine authority to make them leave.

There are so few miracle ministries who have a knockout punch. And there are even fewer who possess the lethal combination jab and hook of potent preaching and mighty miracles.

The greatest crime in many ungodly nations is anti-Christ governments who won't let preachers preach. But the greatest crime in many nations who do allow for freedom of speech are so-called "preachers" who *deny* the power of God. Which crime is greater, I wonder?

Stephen was full of faith and power and performed great wonders and signs among the people (Acts 6:8). *"Great" and "among" describe the power and the place for miracles.* Miracles are to be notable and undeniable in the face of a world whose analysis and data are skeptical and unreliable.

Where are the modern-day miracles that really make us shout and leave the world no doubt? *The doubters couldn't dispute Stephen's miracles so they tried to dispute his message (Acts 6:9-10), but their efforts were futile because Stephen's Spirit-inspired words were as great as his wonders.*

Like hordes of creeping crawlers under a large rock, entire cities are infested with demons who sit comfortably under their cloak of darkness. But see what happens when somebody lifts that rock and allows a laser of bright light to expose those creatures of darkness. They are sent scurrying.

I hear a call for those miracle marshals to come forth. I see mantles of might falling from heaven upon God's chosen. I see beaming lasers of lightning piercing the gross darkness in cities and towns across the world. I hear the booming voice of Jesus Christ calling for the resurrection of the manifold miraculous.

Philip, come forth! Stephen, come forth! Be loosed in the earth! Holy Spirit, give birth! It's time! It's time! It's time to pray and birth forth the miraculous!

CHAPTER 38

CHRISTIAN MARTYRDOM:
THE CHARACTER AND GLORY OF ETERNITY

I believe Stephen was drunk with a spirit of martyrdom. He had lost his life in the crucified and resurrected Christ. He was now living for eternity.

I believe that at the time of Stephen's glorious departure from this earth, the Holy Spirit so saturated him with visions of heaven and glory that it made Stephen count it a privilege to die for Christ (Acts 7:55).

But think about this: Many without Christ possess this spirit of martyrdom. Many die willingly for unrighteous causes without ever having visions of heaven or the glory of God. Some inner-city gangs could be considered fearless martyrs. In many ways, they live a life of complete abandonment. But their martyrdom is born of hate, desperation, and anger. When they die, they leave one hell and enter another. There are no visions of heaven and hopes of glory. How tragic!

And yet how tragic also when you compare today's hell martyr spirit to our own. They die for a lie while many of us can't even live for the truth, much less die for it.

There's a new generation called "Y," who dress in vampire garb and have an obsession with death and darkness. They, too, are not afraid to die. Their perverted identification with death has conquered their fear of it. They've made Satan their friend. You see, they've landed on a scriptural principle. Generation "Y" hates their natural life. That's why they are willing and able to give themselves to Satan's kingdom.

What an eerie perversion and morbid corruption of such a great spiritual truth! The scriptures tell us that one can be a martyr without love (1 Cor. 13:3).

Islamic terrorists who are suicide bombers are a primary example of modern-day martyrs. The promise of paradise and 7 — or is it 70? — virgins who will serve them throughout eternity motivates them to die for their god and their cause. If such demonic deception can lead to such whole-hearted devotion, imagine what the truth in Jesus can do. We need the real martyrdom spirit to infuse the body of Christ.

Think of someone like Evel Knievel, the stunt cyclist. If he doesn't have a spirit of martyrdom and reckless abandonment, I don't know who does. He has no thought for his own body. Yet he does it for fun and a strange kind of entertainment. Getting on a motorcycle and riding it as fast as he can, he endeavors to jump it over 27 cars. Flying through the air before gathered thousands, Evel lands successfully — but not safely — on the other side. The motorcycle tumbles, and Evel rolls, breaking many bones in his body.

I believe anyone who would do that at the risk of his very life is drunk with another spirit. In Evel's case, it is a reckless spirit, with no real eternal purpose. But, in Stephen's case, it was the Holy Spirit.

The Holy Spirit will lead us into utter abandonment for Christ's sake.

As with many martyrs throughout the centuries, Stephen was killed by the religious establishment. Those who passionately stand for the cause of Christ are always persecuted by those who have built their own idea of God.

After Christ Himself, Stephen is considered the first Christian martyr.

Stephen spoke the truth of Jesus Christ. However, his words offended his listeners. They put together a council that brought false witness to the things Stephen was saying (Acts 6:11–13). He proclaimed that God's own people were at fault for suppressing the prophets' call to righteousness. He boldly told them that they were the ones who killed the Holy One, Jesus Christ.

Their reaction was to gnash on him with their teeth. They ran Stephen out of the city and stoned him. Yet Stephen patiently accepted the persecution that was given to him. Stephen asked the Lord not to hold them guilty who had stoned him. He essentially repeated Christ's words on the cross.

This was an extreme act of love. But it takes this sort of extremism to move things for God.

EXTREMISM

Stephen was greatly impacted by the lives and preaching of the early apostles.

Years ago, I was part of an apostolic team of fathers who mentored, equipped, and empowered radical youth. We believed then and still do now that spiritual fathers must define, exemplify, and lead a countercultural movement. It must be our passion to upset the sinful status quo of society and the Church. Youth are key!

In 1933, Hitler said, *"If I can separate the youth of Germany from their parents, I will conquer this nation."* He started a movement called *'The Brown Shirts,'* in which 100,000 youth stood in Berlin with their right hand raised and screaming, "Hitler, we are yours!" Imagine our youth pledging that kind of allegiance to King Jesus!

Around that same time period, the Communist leader Joseph Stalin made the following statement concerning youth: *"If we can effectively kill the national pride and patriotism of just one generation, we will have won that country. Therefore, there must be continued propaganda abroad to undermine the loyalty of the citizens in general and the teenagers in particular. By making readily available drugs of various kinds, by giving a teenager alcohol, by praising his wildness, by strangling him with sex literature, and by advertising to him and her psycho-political preparation, create the necessary attitude of chaos, idleness, and worthlessness."*

If demonically inspired men can affect our youth this way, imagine what divine inspiration will do!

Sin has wasted our youth. We've not given them anything worthy to live for or something worthy to die for. To do anything below what they were created to do will bore them. That is the reason many of our young people turn to drugs, alcohol, immorality, and other sensual thrills. That is why they need to be awakened to their ultimate purpose in Jesus Christ.

In revolutionary countries, youth are trained in combat and weapons. They are taught principles of Communism and the tenets of militant Islam. They give themselves wholeheartedly to the goal of world domination. Someone once said that Satan is preparing his army but that the Church is entertaining her children. We need a radical departure from the standard method of training young men and women for ministry. We need a touch of wholesome extremism to launch a counterculture Jesus revolution!

Yes, just as a certain kind of passivity limits the ministry of God's kingdom, a certain kind of extremism will expand it. The Bible is a book of extremes: Extreme acts of God and history-changing events (like the dividing of the Red Sea and the resurrection of Jesus Christ, among so many others); extreme characters (men and women who changed the world); extreme demands to follow the Lord (denying yourself, taking up your cross daily, etc.); extreme blessings for obedience (Mk. 10:29–30); extreme consequences for unrepentant sin and disobedience (Lk. 13:3, Mt. 7:21–23).

"There has to be an extremism to move things. We need the extremist to start things moving, and we need the balanced teaching to keep them moving in the right direction. We need extreme fervor to launch a movement, but we need the repudiation of extremes to save it from self-destruction. It takes Pentecostal genius to know when and where an extreme doctrine or practice must be modified to a more balanced view — and where, on the other hand, the broad lines of truth must temporarily be narrowed into an extreme emphasis upon one point to ensure a dynamic powerful enough to move things for God. The possession of that uncommon genius marks the God-sent leader who emerged in truly great periods of revival." —Donald Gee

There is little hope for America and many nations of the world without a spiritual revolution. Only a Jesus revolution can bring change – a revolution sent from heaven, with an army of young people trained specifically for the task.

When I speak of a Jesus revolution, I am not speaking of one that will be fought with earthly weapons of destruction or with guns, knives, bullets, and bombs, as in radical Islamic terrorism. It will not be fought with hatred, intimidation, or brute force. No. It will be fought with the gospel, with the love of God, with the power of the Spirit, with radical holiness, with sacrifice, compassion, and courage. It will be a Jesus revolution, an intense clash between two spiritual kingdoms, a heavenly attack on the enemy's strongholds, and a no-compromise stand for morality and truth (This definition was taken from Dr. Michael Brown's *Jesus Manifesto for a Jesus Revolution*).

Here's a prophetic utterance concerning the call to train an army of young people:

"For a new breed of troops to arise, there must be given a new breed of training. For many of my past trainees have only been trained for the easy and the soft and not for the rigorous and the hard. Many have been trained of the letter but not of the Spirit, and so they stand unequipped for the battle and an easy target for the enemy. Sow to the spirit and so shall their swords be sharpened for the flesh has made them dull. For in the flesh is weariness and hands that hang down with the shield of faith. Prepare them to march to a different spirit. Root out the flesh, selfish ambition, and pride and train them to walk by the Lord's side, for the Lord resists the proud but gives grace to the humble.

"The training must be accurate and precise, according to calling and grace. Do not seek to make them what they are not, but help them find what they are: According to calling and grace, not color or race, everyone in their place. Then shall they learn to use their weapons and overcome the enemy.

"And be careful to remember that the trainee is only as good as the trainer. Be skillful in your training, and learn to use the word of God

*with precision and accuracy, holding forth the word of life and being a
shining example of a doer of that word.*

*"And as a good army officer knows well the different phases of
training, so know the end of one phase and the beginning of another.
Know the readiness of your troops and the ability I've placed in each one.
Prove them and know that they are soldiers fit to fight."*

Here is another prophetic utterance concerning America and the
training of these young men, referred to as "special forces."

*"America will come upon hard times. Many hearts will open, and the
gospel will penetrate into the cities of America. Revival will sweep the
land even as it is being judged. Young men who will be trained and ready
will be as special forces, and they will run with fire in their feet and in
their hearts. They will be free of care and family ties and at a moment's
notice will respond to the Spirit's call and go. When the enemy unleashes
his onslaught on the cities of America, these shall be ready. They will be
sent to the battle equipped as troops for the trenches, where victories are
won. Unconventional wisdom and special skill shall be given them for
conquest, and they will go armed to suffer for their Lord and
Commander-in-Chief.*

*"These special forces shall be men who have no desire for their own
glory but seek only the glory of Him who sends them. They are men with
no hidden agendas or secret plans — only to advance the kingdom.*

*"This ministry shall be one that the Lord shall use to prepare some of
these special troops. Prepare them to go. Prepare them to stand. Prepare
them to speak. Prepare them to fight. Equip them to avoid casualties, to
endure hardships, and to be strong and courageous."*

A call to arms is going out to the young and the brave. A call to
arms is sounding to summon the bold and the daring to come and
fight in the greatest spiritual battle of all time. With the
consummation of the ages drawing closer, the war for men's souls is
intensifying. A new breed of Christian soldier must be born.

One of the critical needs of the hour is for qualified, radical laborers to be equipped for service, laborers who love God and are established in His Word, trained in the essentials of the great commission, ablaze with revival fire, and ready to lay down their lives for the gospel — men and women of character and power.

May the Lord raise up a new courageous and wholly consecrated generation full of the Word and full of the Spirit who will serve Him by life or by death (Phil. 1:20). May this new breed come forth to work the works of God in the earth and be able to boldly declare: *"For to me, to live is Christ, and to die is gain."* (Phil: 1:21).

PRAYER OF CONSECRATION

Holy Father,

I have tried to do your will and failed.

Now, by your grace, I come to place in your care my all.

I will to be yours.

I will to do your will.

I will to believe you and obey you.

I will to know your will as revealed in thy Word.

I will to be led by the Spirit of truth.

I will to let your Holy Spirit help me to subdue all that is contrary to your will into your hands.

I will to trust your Holy Spirit to bring to maturity the graces that you have adorned my life with.

I acknowledge my own helplessness in conforming to your will.

In weakness I come to you, and I surrender my all to you.

And now, dear Lord, I lay my all on your altar.

I can do no more.

All is yours, and what is yours, you can use or lay aside.

All glory, honor, and praise to you Eternal Father and Glorious Lord!

ABOUT THE AUTHOR

Bert M. Farias, together with his wife, Carolyn, graduates of Rhema Bible Training Center, founded Holy Fire Ministries in 1997 after serving for nine years as missionaries in West Africa, establishing nation-changing interdenominational Bible training centers with an organization called Living Word Missions.

From 1999 to 2003, Bert served as the internship coordinator on the senior leadership team of the Brownsville Revival School of Ministry and Fire School of Ministry in Pensacola, Florida, a school birthed from a massive, heaven-sent revival that brought approximately four million visitors from around the world, with an estimated 150,000 first-time conversions. There, Rev. Farias and his wife taught and mentored young men and women in the call of God and trained them for the work of the ministry.

Bert is a messenger of the Lord carrying a spirit of revival to the Church and the nations. An anointing of fire marks his ministry with frequent demonstrations of the Spirit and the power of God. With a divine commission to also write, Bert has authored several books with an emphasis on helping to restore the true spirit of Christianity in the Church today and preparing the saints for the glory of God, the harvest, and the imminent return of the Lord.

Before being dedicated solely to the full-time preaching and teaching ministry, Bert experienced a unique and powerful baptism of fire. His consuming passion is for human beings to come into a real and vibrant relationship with the Lord Jesus Christ through the power of the Holy Spirit and to become passionate workers in His kingdom, thus preparing them for the second coming of Christ, being among the wise virgins and a part of the first-fruits harvest who will gain an abundant entrance into glory and receive a sure reward.

Bert currently resides in Windham, New Hampshire, with his beautiful wife, Carolyn. They are proud parents of one precious son of promise.

MINISTRY INFORMATION

To become a monthly partner with Holy Fire Ministries, to schedule a speaking engagement with Bert and/or Carolyn, to receive a free monthly newsletter, or to follow Bert's blog, please visit our website: **www.holy-fire.org**

HOLY FIRE MINISTRIES

PO Box 4527

Windham, NH 03087

Email: adm@holy-fire.org

OTHER BOOKS BY BERT M. FARIAS

SOULISH LEADERSHIP

PURITY OF HEART

THE JOURNAL OF A JOURNEY TO HIS HOLINESS

THE REAL SPIRIT OF REVIVAL

THE REAL SALVATION

THE REAL GOSPEL

MY SON, MY SON

PRAYER: THE LANGUAGE OF THE SPIRIT

*To order any of these books or to view a synopsis of them, visit our website or Amazon books.

*If this book or any of Bert's other books has been a blessing to you, kindly post a review on Amazon.

Made in the USA
Columbia, SC
14 May 2018